IMAGINE A EINE
CITY VOR,
WHERE YOU
CAN DO N
AS NNST,
YOU PLEASE LST

# IMAGINE A CITY WHERE YOU CAN DISCOVER YOURSELF, DECEXPERIENCE YOURSELF.

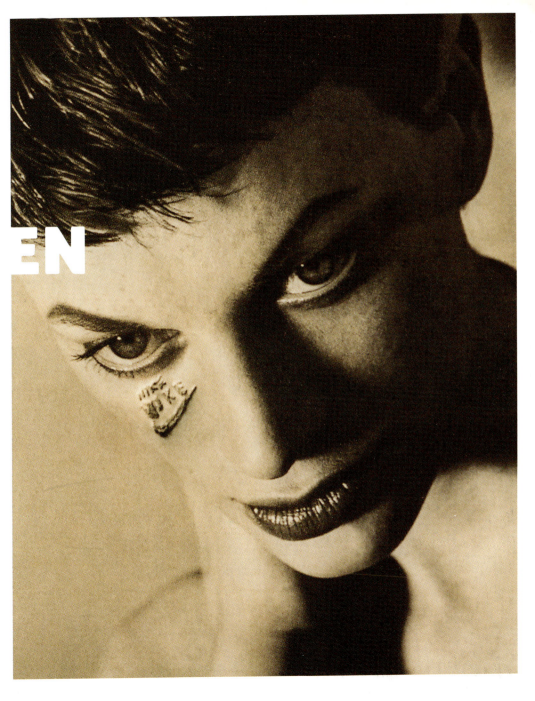

IMAGINER VOR
A CITY TADT
WHOSE IE
REALITŸ IS TH
OF A MARKETI
ILLUSION.

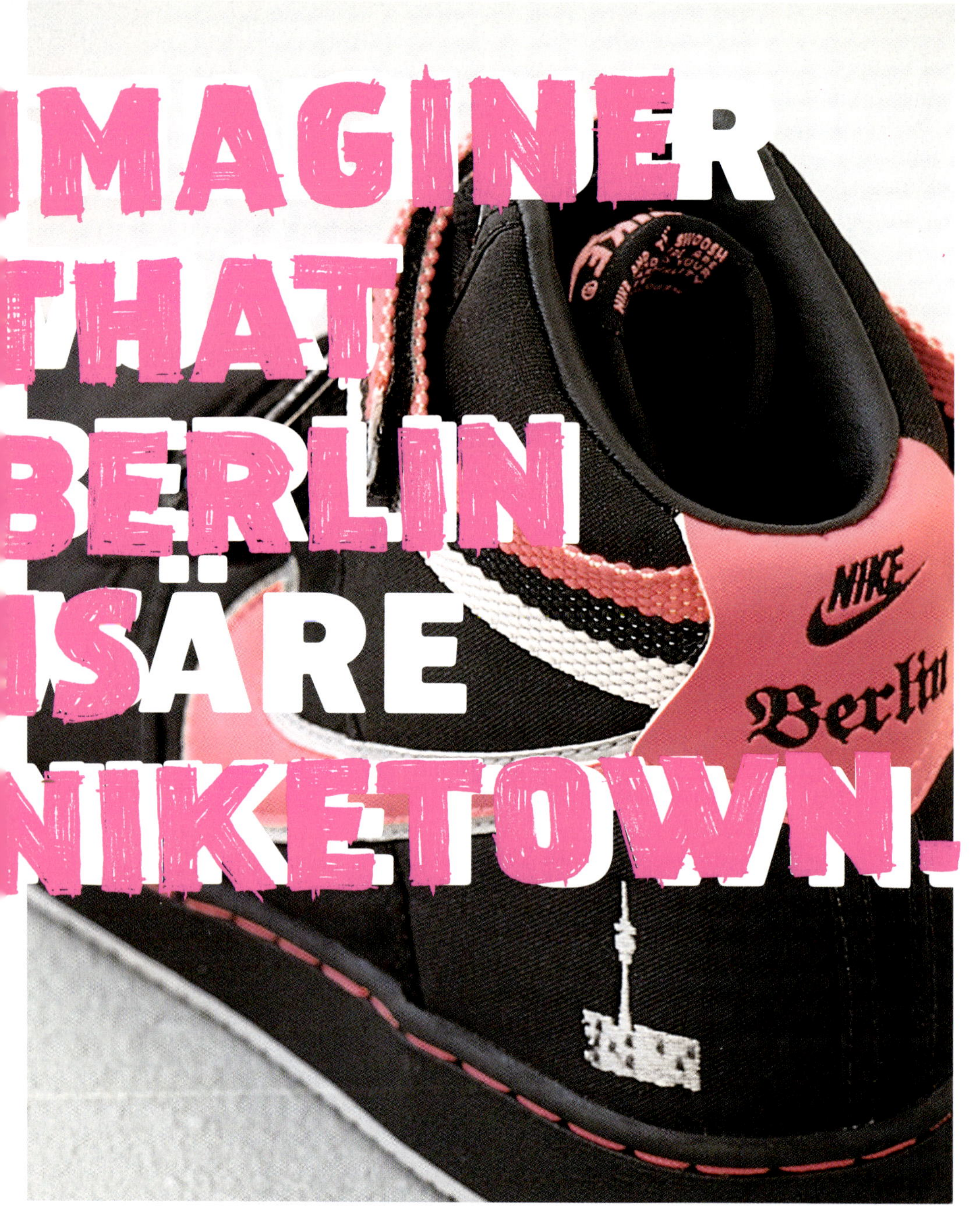
IMAGINE
THAT
BERLIN
IS
NIKETOWN.
NIKE
Berlin

# WHO'S AFRAID NIKE TO

# NIKE URBANISM, BRANDING AND THE CITY OF TOMORROW

Friedrich von Borries

episode publishers
Rotterdam, 2004

14

# PREFACE

In the 1970s, Manfredo Tafuri exhaustively analyzed how the avant-garde is continually absorbed by Capitalism. At that time, if recollection serves, he did not yet speak about Situationism. Friedrich von Borries shows how firms such as Nike have appropriated the anti-Capitalist methods and strategies of the Situationists. Occasionally, these stories challenge credulity – when, for example, Nike organizes demonstrations and protest campaigns against its own products. In relating all of this, Borries is not merely factual and analytical; he also takes advantage of such true implausibilities and implausible truth in order to journey with the reader on speculative excursions into the future. It is precisely through this approach that his detailed analyses of actual marketing strategies in the urban realm gain their strength.

In this book, Friedrich von Borries demonstrates step by step how a sport shoe (one could almost say: a somewhat inconsequential product) has transformed the city into an experiential space. The future brand city will not be only (or perhaps even: no longer) a city of logos, taking the form of ever larger illuminated advertisements, more striking buildings that house corporate headquarters, more and larger urban entertainment centers. Although this type of city will not disappear in the near future, it seems to me that it already belongs to a different era, one in which the media still functioned as broadcasters.

The new brand city described by Borries is far more than this. It is a dynamic city, a setting for organizing 'situations.' In order to reach even the smallest target groups, the media will be deployed in this city far more interactively than they are today. Streets, fallow zones, interstitial spaces and ruins will play essential roles in the brand name city. These spaces will not be overlaid with advertising in classical fashion, but will instead become the objects of discriminating marketing strategies. Here initiatives from below that devise new leisure activities will be instrumentalized, as will critical actions and political demonstrations.

The new brand city is all-encompassing, permeating and enveloping the urban realm like the pliable sport shoes described by Borries at the beginning of his text. And just as these shoes, as they age, assume the shapes, sweat and smell of the feet occupying them, the brands respond to urban life. Friedrich von Borries is able, in his persuasive an-aly-sis, to bring this reality before our eyes in astonishingly concrete form – no small achievement. The thematics of *Who's Afraid of Niketown* come very close to the problematic dealt with in Howard Rheingold's book *Smart Mobs, The Next Social Revolution*, which caused a sensation. Rheingold deals with new forms of social organization that are gener-ated, he argues, primarily by the new wireless media. We know that the technological acceleration of organizational forms has implications for the organization of the city and of architecture. Like Borries, Rheingold begins his analysis of the contemporary city in the streets (in this case, those of Tokyo), where he observes novel behavioral patterns. Rheingold's analysis of the new technologies is convincing, but at the same time his book remains vague, a fact that bears a precise relevance to the fact that he is now regarded by many people as a guru: For gurus, vagueness can be efficacious. Friedrich von Borries has no need to roam. Instead, he remains focused upon familiar locales. He remains at home in Berlin, close to his own biography, and standing on his own two feet. And precisely for this reason, his analysis attains its extreme precision.

Bart Lootsma

# INTRODUCTION

I usually wear sneakers. White ones from Adidas, orange ones from Saucony, black ones from Nike. This book on the influence of branding on urban space, then, is hardly the work of a disinterested observer, but instead of a consumer, a member of a target group. I am part of the system I observe and describe.[1] This does not prevent me from practicing a system-immanent type of criticism, from critiquing certain contemporary manifestations of consumer society – despite my fundamental acceptance of how consumption is a constitutive element of our society, of how strategies of consumption make vital contributions to constructions of individual identity and individual representation.

The city of Niketown Berlin imagined earlier does not actually exist; it is a projection into the future. But is it really so implausible? Or does it already exist, if not as a reality, then at least as a potentiality? Do we find auguries in the present of the emergence of such a city? And what would this mean for our understanding of and our dealings with the city as we find it today? It is a question, then, of detecting contemporary processes of formation. Just as archaeologists speculate about past epochs, conceived as unities, based on ancient fragments and shards he chances across, and derives pictures of such past times, this book attempts to gain access to a possible future by using fragments of the present day. The focus is on one partial dimension of the present. Just as with an excavation, the search begins with a previously delimited section, as we search for traces within a restricted field, aware that these traces represent only one possibility for comprehending our own time. The instrumentalization of the urban realm in the context of marketing strategies is only a small section of the multifarious processes of transformation to which urban space is exposed in the wake of advancing globalization. But precisely via this section, as though through a magnifying glass, we are in a position to perceive such contemporary developments more distinctly and to better understand them.

Ever since we have become aware of working conditions in the Asian sweatshops, Nike has symbolized exploitation and global injustice. This aspect of Nike has been dealt with exhaustively. This book reverses perspectives within the discourse on globalization by investigating the influence of marketing strategies – and the sociocultural developments associated with them – on our local habitat. It undertakes a process of introspection, investigating which possible futures might emerge in our cities in the context of Nike's urban interventions.

Classical Modernism assigned architects and architecture with a moral-pedagogical task, one resting upon an idealistic worldview, and entailing the striving for a new, egalitarian social order. The dream of classical Modernism in architecture (one that made a profound impression on a generation of contemporary architects) was to create space for this new reality. But in recent years, the actual task of architecture has changed radically. The illusion machine of marketing has rediscovered the reality: architecture is now intended to convey the identity of a brand, is now expected, as an experiential realm, to be an element in brand communication. From this premise, architecture and urban planning acquire a new concept of functionality, one that fundamentally alters the self-image of architects, planners and designers alike, along with the scope of their responsibilities.

# NIKE URBANISM – BERLIN ON THE WAY TO NIKETOWN

Nike is to be found on the various levels of the city: First of all on feet, then in display windows, on posters, in advertisements appearing in city magazines, in fashion reports, as subway stickers. Why, then, search for Nike? As a globally active enterprise, Nike pursues differing advertising strategies within its various markets, while at the same time striving to communicate an identical brand identity worldwide. Using Berlin as an example, we can demonstrate how brand identities are experience-able, and are hence communicated, through interventions in urban space, how the activation of urban space functions as an instrument of marketing. Berlin is a European testing laboratory, a place of openness and enthusiasm for experimentation. Berlin is a melting pot of various target groups, possesses an active subculture and has the image of being future-oriented and trendy.[2] Many actions that are possible here, and which have been embraced by target groups, could not be implemented with such conceptual clarity in other European cities (with the exception of London). To search for Nike in Berlin, hence, means to discover a piece of the future here.

THE BOLZPLATZ: Berlin, summer 1999: With the Bolzplatz campaign, Nike makes its entrance into the public space of the city. In Berlin, there are many playgrounds equipped with facilities for playing soccer, the so-called 'Bolzplätze.' The Bolzplätze are simple paved playing fields for soccer with little gates and high metal fences to prevent balls from flying away. They are reminiscent of pictures showing basketball courts in the Bronx, the birthplace of hip hop culture, as familiar from music videos and television films. The Bolzplätze in Berlin are not especially well utilized, but instead are seen as outworn, rejected spaces. In summer of 1999, under the aegis of the slogan "Freedom lies behind the fence," Nike attempted to transform these Bolzplätze into animated brand spaces. Hung throughout the city were large-format posters mapping the locations of the various Bolzplätze.

Little stickers with the inscription 'to the nearest Bolzplatz' done in the neon colors of a magic marker aesthetic were adhered to lamp-posts and power boxes. On the high fences of the Bolzplätze were signs imitating those bearing officious prohibitions worded in phrases like: "Enter at your own risk" and "No bottles" (the German word for bottle, 'Flasche', has the connotation of loser, failure). None of the signs, stickers or posters bore the name Nike, only the word Berlin and the Swoosh graphic appeared as the logo of Niketown Berlin. The presence of the campaign in public space was reinforced by advertisements in the locally based media. In movie spots, young people kicked on the Bolzplätze together with stars from Hertha BSC (Berlin's most famous soccer club), while on the 'Fuck You' hotline of the youth station Kiss FM, where youth ridicule their elders, insult their teachers, or just vent their frustrations, the topics of soccer and public space were thematized in feigned appeals from soccer fanatics and adversaries.

In the wake of the campaign, the Bolzplätze were used so intensively by Berlin youth that during the following summer, the municipal administration supervising Berlin's green spaces were prompted to install genuine prohibition signs containing house rules and reminding users of the ordinances governing periods of quiet.

BATTLE OF THE DISTRICTS: In summer 2000 came the continuation of the Bolzplatz campaign, the Battle of the Districts. Teams played against one another, with young people assembled to do battle for their respective districts. In the K. O. system, teams played first in the individual districts on each local Bolzplatz, after which the winners of the multi-district finale were announced. The battle of the districts was coordinated with district administrators and school officials. According to Nike, 550 teams consisting of seven individuals each signed up for the campaign. "We wanted to provide the Berlin street kickers with a platform to compete in a sportsmanlike manner. As centers for sport, creativity and youth culture, the Bolzplätze were the most appropriate locales for such street soccer tournaments. The idea of having districts matched against one another is based on the emphatic pride of the individual districts among Berlin's youth. If you ask young

# "FREEDOM LIES BEHIND THE FENCE"

Bolzplatz campaign, Berlin 1999

ple where they come from, they identify themselves first and forest as residents of Kreuzberg, Lichtenberg or Charlottenburg,"claims
. ...e.[3]

The campaign posters took up the aesthetics of graffiti and Japanese
Manga. Pithy phrases like "There are no rules" and "WE: the left-overs"
convey the image of street fighters who match their strengths in soccer.
Accordingly, teams bore names such as Killers or Westend Tigers,
which are reminiscent of familiar Berlin youth gangs such as the Grant
Master Fighters from Wedding, a typical Berlin working class district.
[Cf. Goddar 2000]

SUBGROUND BATTLE: "Soccer Basketball Skate-
boarding underground" was the slogan of Subground Battle, a three day
long action taking place in September 2001[4], which transformed the
disused underground station below the Reichstag into a Nike experiential
space. In contrast to previous campaigns, which had concentrated on
soccer, this one now included basketball and skateboarding. Just as
with the Battle of the Districts, teams representing individual Berlin
districts competed against one another in various sports. Participants
could test their abilities and acquire points at several stations. In the
area of soccer, there were competitive activities such as volleying, skill
contests or shot velocity measurement. Altogether, 2000 teenagers took
part in the event.

As a mysterious deserted space lying below the ground level of the
city, the underground station was converted according to the functional
requirements of the respective sport activities. For the skaters, the
underground tube became a pipe; for basketball players, the representative hall area became an arena. The introduction of security fences
underscored the character of spontaneous appropriation or occupation
dreamed of by every skater. Slogans such as "When skateboarding
becomes a crime, it goes underground" alluded to the experiences and
the desires of young skaters vis-à-vis public spaces such as the
underground system. Everything is forbidden, nothing sanctioned. An
unused urban space is liberated by Nike from the habitual structures of
control and transformed into a space of experience, and moreover en-

tirely 'under the Reichstag,' a highly charged symbol of German history, and today the seat of the legislative power. Subground Battle under the Reichstag. With Nike, everything is completely different. So just do it.

The accompanying campaign did not restrict outdoor advertising to the classical poster, but instead attempted to reach target groups via their various sports activities. For the skateboarders, hence, manhole covers were affixed with stickers, while for the basketball players, the hoops in public playing courts became advertising surfaces. Just as, in the context of the Bolzplatz campaign, prohibition signs offered ironic commentary on everyday urban restrictions, now faked traffic signs referred to everyday functionality, so hostile to sports and fun. 200 signs [ADC 2002, p. 508] hang upside-down, thereby symbolically pointing towards the Subground Battle, were mounted throughout the city and endowed the event with an urban presence transcending its actual location, taking effect in an urban medial environment beyond the actual site involved.

The Subground Battle united the features of both previous interventions: The staging and recoding of a locale, as in the Bolzplatz campaign, and the amplification of already existing potentialities for identification via the parasitic superimposition of Nike's brand image.

SECRET TOURNAMENT: A ship lies in a harbor by night, while small speedboats ferry the fighters on board. There are 24 soccer players[5], the best in the world (or at least the best among those who have contracts with Nike). This old freighter is the setting for the Secret Tournament, the leitmotif of Nike's campaign for the World Cup 2002. In the belly of the ship is a cage, with three against three, and no goalie: Whoever scores a goal, first wins. Eric Cantona is the grandmaster. Like a prison guard, he tosses the ball through a hole from above into the cage of the gladiators. Only the technically perfect player could possibly win in this constricted space, a player who has mastered all the tricks and simultaneously enjoys instantaneous communication with both of his teammates. The losers will be thrown overboard, for in this world, there is no place for losers. In the finale, Os Tornados[6], consisting of Roberto Carlos, Luis Figo and Ronaldo, are opposed by 'Triple

PRECISELY AS POE
IDEOLOGIES AND R
EXPLANATORY MO
DUCTING OUR LIVE
TO US HOW THE WO
OF HYPERCAPITAL

UST DO IT. LETS R
AND THE LOSERS G

TICAL

ELIGIONS OFFER

DELS FOR CON-

S, NIKE EXPLAINS

RLD

SM FUNCTIONS.


LL,

O OFF.

Espresso,' composed of Thierry Henry, Francesco Totti and Hidetoshi Nakata. Triple Espresso wins by means of a trick. Francesco Totti bends down and looks as though he is tying his shoelace. Even before Cantona releases the ball from his hand, Henry takes off, using Totti as a springboard. The ball has barely passed through the small porthole in the ceiling of the cage when Henry flies toward it, butting it across half of the playing field and into the goal with his head. Not exactly fair play, but equally not a violation of the rules. A clever trick, a creative approach to gaining the advantage in a tournament. The final words of the film, spoken off camera in the darkness of the night while three human forms are shown being tossed into the water, are "the losers go off": Total selection. Precisely as political ideologies and religions offer explanatory models for conducting our lives, Nike explains to us how the world of Hypercapitalism functions: in the case of Nike, a remorseless battle that produces heroes. Just do it. Lets roll. And the losers go off.

SCORPION K.O.: Berlin, 2002. The Secret Tournament spot is reenacted for the teenaged target group as an experiential space. A tour rolls through Germany, the Nike Scorpion KO tournament, with a finale in Berlin; Nikepark and Subground under the Reichstag. The posters for the tour show the international teams of three in a simplified stenciled graffiti aesthetic. A bus, styled like an American prison transport van, transfers spectators and players from the Reichstag to Niketown and Nikepark. A tourist shuttle, in theme park style, as a generator of identification. Just as in the spot, the teams compete against one another in cages. And the 'losers' go off.

Phil McAveety, director of marketing for Nike in Europe, the Middle East and Africa, refers to the campaign as "one of the most innovative and most interlocked soccer campaigns Nike has created to date" [press statement, Nike 2002]. Here, various elements are linked together, including a spot (which can be downloaded from the Nike website free of charge), music (the remix of Elvis Presley's A Little Bit of Conversation reached the top 10 in the US charts), interactive media (a computer game was set up on the Nike website), and experiential spaces (parallel to the World Cup, there were Nikeparks in 13 cities).

**NIKEPARK:** Berlin 2000; the European soccer championship is being held in Belgium and the Netherlands. Nikepark takes shape on the location of the former 'Stadion der Weltjugend' (Stadium of World Youth) in Berlin-Mitte. The Stadion der Weltjugend was constructed in 1950 on the site of a former barracks, and was inaugurated as the 'Walter Ulbricht Stadium,' named after the leader of the GDR. After his fall and on occasion of the 10th 'Weltjugend-spiele' (World Youth Festival), a kind of Eastern European Woodstock, it was renamed the Stadion der Weltjugend. This Stadion der Weltjugend was a place with a distinct GDR history, heavily laden with the symbolism of the FDGB (Free German Trade Unions, the official trade union of the GDR) and FDJ (Free German Youth, the official youth organisation), that is to say, not just a place of sport, but also of political remembrance. In keeping with the predominant practice of the 1990s, according to which places associated with the GDR past were effaced from the urban realm, the Stadion der Weltjugend was demolished, and the premises cleared in 1994. Subsequently, the site lay fallow, and as a consequence of an unsuccessful application for the Olympic Games of 2000, was never rebuilt as planned. The former Stadion der Weltjugend is a place with high symbolic content, one we experience as a wasteland, an unused symbolic territory, authorized for occupation. Into this breach sprang Nike, opening its Berlin Nikepark[7] to coincide with the European soccer championship of 2000, as a locus for its urban marketing activities. Radio spots, spliced into radio ads in the style of pirate broadcasts with static noise, announced the arrival of underground soccer fighters – stars like Edgar Davids and Oliver Bierhoff. Since then, the former Stadion der Weltjugend has become – as Nikepark – a fixed component of Nike's campaigns. From the Stadion der Weltjugend – a venue for diverse youth games, rallies for world peace and FDJ events – emerged Nikepark. Here, brand identity is presented as a form of freedom and resistance, as though the consumption of lifestyles and their products were our political counter-model to real existing socialism. The public hand is not in a position to (or does not care to) approach the site of memory known as the Stadion der Weltjugend with an adequate substitute, but instead allows this symbolic place to be occupied by a locally operating global player. This incapacity to deal productively with the symbolism of the GDR gives rise to a new, fatal symbolism: that of economic interests.

**NIKE PALACE:** Berlin 2002, the 'Palast der Republik' (Palace of the Republic). The inability to discover a matter-of-fact, natural mode for dealing with the symbolic sites of the GDR [cf. Koolhaas 2004] leads to an additional, intriguing interaction between Berlin and Nike. There exists no more symbolically charged location in Berlin than the Palast der Republik. During the GDR era, the Palast der Republik, set on the site of the former Royal Palace, was a socialist pleasure dome, and, as the seat of the GDR-Parliament, a representative building of that state. After Reunification, the Palast was almost demolished because of asbestos contamination, and has remained disused ever since. For some time now, the dream has circulated through Berlin's club scene of using the empty Palast der Republik for cultural purposes in the Berlin tradition of temporary occupations. After a decision on the part of the Bundestag to completely demolish the Palast and rebuild the Royal Palace there, an association was formed [www.zwischenpalastnutzung.de] for the purpose of planning and organizing temporary use of the GDR building. Urban Catalyst, a group of researchers from Berlin's Technical University, which is preoccupied with the conversion and reactivation of fallow urban surfaces, was entrusted with preparing a feasibility study. As the sponsor for the necessary security measures in the amount of 1.2 million Euros, Nike was approached by the initiators. In exchange, Nike was offered the right of first use. Prior to its temporary use by various cultural agencies of the Berlin scene, the Palast became a Nike experiential space for a period of two weeks. [Cf. Poganatz/Schwegmann 2002] Imagine: In place of the Palast der Republik emerged the Nike Palace, with the Swoosh logo usurping the place of GDR coat of arms. Welcome to Niketown!

**NIKETOWN:** If we compare the possible transformation of the Palast der Republik into Nike Palace with the transformation of the former Stadion der Weltjugend into Nikepark, the difference between signifiers is conspicuous. While the

Stadium was originally intended to be a place of sports, the Palast der Republik had always been – like the Royal Palace – a locus for the demonstration and exercise of power. And while it is easy to imagine a manufacturer of sportswear redesigning a location associated with sports activities, there is something appalling about the notion of a global player taking possession of an architectural symbol of domination from a failed state. And yet it is precisely this instance of the architecture of authority, a remnant of a collapsed state, one associated with repression and lack of freedom, that furnishes an effective backdrop for the staging of Just do it philosophy. Just do it, the message of Nike, can be expressed in the Palast der Republik if the impression can be conveyed that the spirit of sportsmanlike liberty has now supplanted the symbolism of domination. Then the Silent Revolution of the GDR becomes further evidence of Just do it philosophy, and the palace of a perished republic bears witness to its superiority. Nike Palace becomes a symbol of the victory of the capitalist commodity system over socialist Utopia, of the individual over the collective, testifying that not the principle of the constitutional state was the key motivation of the propagandists of the Silent Revolution, but instead the allure of the glittering display of consumer articles. For the time being at least, there will be no Nike Palace in Berlin. Shortly before the opening of the exhibition 'Zwischenpalast-nutzung' (featuring proposed temporary uses for the palace) in the adjacent former 'Staatsratsgebäude' (Privy Council Building), Nike withdrew from the project when indiscretions revealed their interest in sponsoring temporary use of the building. [Cf. Poganatz/Schwegmann 2002] Independently of whether there is to be a Nike Palace in the Palast der Republik or not (perhaps Nike will indeed display interest in the idea once again; the future of the Palast der Republik remains uncertain), the very possibility of such a transformation is already illuminating.

Just as the Royal Palace was an expression of the claims to authority of the Prussian monarchy, the Palast der Republik was an expression of the GDR's ideology of domination. The conjecture obtrudes that a Nike Palace would be an expression of our society's self-image. But do Nike and the other global players exercise authority? Is the dissolution of a political symbolic space by a brand space a symptom of the dissolution of political discourse by a multiplicity of brand identities? Does the Nike Palace symbolize the relationship between a political-economic order and its citizenry? Or does it symbolize the dissolution of state authority by the domination of a globalized economy? If we reflect upon both forms of transformation presented here, both involving the conversion of politically connoted urban spaces into experiential brand spaces, then it becomes clear that the principle of transformation is a subtle and logically consequential strategy of branding. Via references to a pre-existing set of conditions, via negative references, the Nike brand space can set itself off from the merely existence as a space of freedom and limitless possibilities. Both the past and the insufficient present day become material for creating a contrast with a positive fiction of a better brand world. But precisely through this maneuver, and because it takes advantage of the language of power, the new space becomes an architecture of authority. Would such a global player – particularly one that has come to symbolize the inequalities of globalization and to function as the bogeyman of the anti-globalization movement – dare to be associated with a symbol of state authority? It may even be that the danger represented by such an obvious proximity to power and authority is the real reason why Nike decided to distance itself from an opportunity to sponsor a project for temporary use. Since Nike is already quite powerful, and consistently deploys subtle forms of authority, it may be just as well not to put these on display. With Nikepark, the portends are different, since here, Nike had to delimit itself not primarily from the GDR past, but instead from the inability of the public hand to organize public space in such a way that it answers present day needs for spontaneous occupation and temporary scenarization. In Nikepark, Nike is the better good, while in the context of Nike Palace, Nike would have merely been the better ruler.

In modernity, as Horkheimer/Adorno demonstrate in their disquisition on the culture industry, authority does not mean power over bodies, but instead over thought. "The ruler no longer says: You must think as I do or else die. He says: You are free not to think as I do, your life, your property, everything will remain in your possession. But from this day henceforth, you become a stranger among us." [Tocqueville, cited by

Horkheimer/Adorno, 1989] A contemporary architecture of authority, then, no longer represents the omnipotence of the system in relation to the nullity of the isolated individual, but is rather expressed to the extent that it possesses the power to define life and to influence the shaping of our lifestyles. The brand identity today bestows a sense of homeland, because it makes bids for identification available, along with the very spaces within which newly won identities may be tested, experienced and acculturated. When speaking of the classical architecture of authority, we mean representation, that is to say, the depiction of a cultural self-image and the power relations prevailing within a given society. The new architecture of authority symbolizes not oppression, but rather delimits those invisible boundaries within which the free choice of identities and lifestyles can fulfill itself, defining the space of needs and desires. This is not repression, but rather seduction. "The development of these desires for being seen, for accessories, for self-staging, are the foundations of a new, practically unlimited exploitation. On their basis, consumption becomes a performance, while to lead a life overwhelmed by stress and over-commitment becomes a positive duty." [Böhme 2001, p. 82] The new architecture of authority, of brand experience, is an aestheticized space within which freedom and limitless possibilities are staged.

In the interventions described above, fallow public spaces – the neglected Bolzplätze, the empty, stripped down Palast der Republik, the disused U-Bahn station – are activated and scenarized as experiential spaces. Selected conceptions such as those of battle and underground, as well as via the graphics deployed, for example graffiti, summon associations with the radical protest movements. Such allusions to the culture of protest are aimed at the unease felt in regimented cities, while the scenarization of protest is a bid for identification. Urban space is transformed into a brand environment that, as an experiential space, conveys the brand identity of Nike. In these three campaigns, something new and different flashes out, something that compels us to take a closer look, to reflect. All of these campaigns depart from familiar advertising styles; they are more persuasive, more striking. In contrast to the multiplicity of events (street soccer, streetball etc.), familiar from brands such as Adidas and Puma, these interventions seem to transmit the identity of Nike more insistently. And in contrast to the familiar brand experience parks and flagship stores, these urban interventions are more flexible, more rapid, more reactive.

These interventions allude to a future city whose patterns of use are impressed by brand specific scenarizations. The name of a city that would embody the image of Nike would be 'Niketown.' But Niketown is not a city, but instead a large sporting goods store. Worldwide, there are 18 of them, located in Atlanta, Berlin, Boston, Eugene, Chicago, Denver, Honolulu, Las Vegas, London, Los Angeles, Melbourne, Miami, New York, Orange County, Portland, San Francisco, Seattle, and Toronto. The première European Niketown opened in Berlin in 1999, followed by Niketown London. At first glance, the Berlin Niketown is a department for sporting goods that sells only the firm's products, as in every flagship store. But Niketown is something more. The building is subdivided into pavilions, each assigned a different theme. In each pavilion, devotionalia of great sports heroes are displayed, while sports scenes are shown on projection screens. Unlike, for example, the Adidas Original Stores or the Puma Concept Stores, it is not a question of opening cost-effective paths of distribution that project a persuasive atmosphere. In fact, there is no financial gain involved in selling sports articles on location in the Niketowns. The Niketowns were erected primarily to endow the spirit of Nike with a place where the spirit of Nike could be experienced. Hence, for example, 50 percent of the store surface in New York is devoted to exhibitions, that is to say, to shoes, rackets, and articles of clothing once worn by Nike athletes.

The real-existing Niketowns are often characterized as temples or cathedrals. [Cf. Binder 2002, p. 17] To begin with, this is false typologically, since their interior organizations play with the motifs of square, street and district, not with the typologies of sacral spaces. But it also misconceives the strategy actually being exploited. From Niketown, the city can be conquered and discovered. Here, actions can be organized and coordinated that allow the city to experienced differently: In London the sightseeing run, in New York the running schools. In Berlin too, Niketown is a point of departure for urban interventions. Young people pick up

Bolzplatz stickers from Niketown, the ones they affix to lamp-posts in order to play at being urban partisans or guerillas, demarcating the stomping grounds of their own districts, and signing up at Niketown for various battles. Already in the campaign for the opening of Niketown Berlin, Nike formulated a counter-image to the existing city, describing a new city that would be freer, less controlled, more spontaneous. But this city must first be fought for, conquered, and Nike lays claim to the role of organizing resistance against the regimentation of the city, presenting itself as an actual resistance movement. This is made explicit by the posters for the opening of Niketown Berlin, using the graphics and simple resources typical of the protest movements of the late 1960s and 1970s: Torn out pictorial fragments, texts assembled from individual elements, pieces of adhesive tape. In terms of content, the campaign thematizes prohibitions within the urban realm. Slogans such as "It is strictly forbidden not to play on the grass" express the everyday experiences of the young target group (that in fact, everything is prohibited, nothing permitted) and anticipate disobedience and resistance. Consistent with this style, the posters were not applied to expensive advertising surfaces, but instead in construction zones and on the concrete anchors of construction site barriers. Even the slogan of the Bolzplatz campaign ("freedom lies behind the fence") plays ambiguously on the omnipresent structures of urban prohibition, simultaneously referring to the cool image of the criminality indigenous to the real basketball courts in the Bronx. The Battle of the Districts propagated a genre of soccer that does not adhere to the rules of classical club sports, but instead to those of the street. Nike's goal is to associate club independent street soccer with Nike's brand identity. The motto for this, 'Freestyle,' reappears in the campaigns of 2002 and 2003. The advertising or activation campaign[8] thereby adapts methods that had been evolved and applied by sub-cultural movements: Graffiti, fake media guerillas, campaigns à la action art. As a global player, Nike seizes upon the aesthetics of street culture and the subversive youth movement in Berlin. Nike attempts to synthesize an image of resistance against urban repression, and to this end, copies the strategies of the urban guerillas of the 1970s. In this fictive Niketown, the marketing guerilla assumes the status of the urban guerilla. In Nike's interventions into the city, it becomes possible to experience this fictive Niketown.

The Niketowns also serve a double function. As real buildings, they act as tourist attractions, each ranking high on the list of most-frequented sightseeing destinations in its respective city. [Cf. Gunter/Inaba 2001] In them, visitors can shop while admiring icons of contemporary sports culture. In this sense, Berlin is the ideal location for a Niketown, since Nike's brand image coincides at many points with that of the German capital: Berlin before the fall of the Wall as an outpost of freedom; Berlin during the breaching and fall of the Wall as a city of upheaval and liberation; Berlin after the fall of the Wall as the metropolis of new cultural departures, a home to variegated and fascinating subcultures. The Niketowns anchor a global player to various local micro-structures, to which (no differently from other experiential brand spaces) the core values of the brand can be directly transmitted in spatial terms, rather than merely through the media. Simultaneously, Niketown is an emblem for a new type of city. The ideal, imaginary Niketown provides a counter-image to the contemporary city, because it constitutes an image of an experientially dense and ungovernable city. In its campaigns, Nike anticipates protests against the regimentation of the modern, functionalist city, generating an image of resistance. Sports and an imaginary protest against unfreedom are fused in a brand image. In its various temporary interventions, Nike attempts to render this idealized Niketown susceptible to real experience. The specific Niketown, then, is only the spatially and organizational point of departure for these actions. Nike's interventions activate fallow urban spaces and recontextualize them as intensive Nike experiential spaces.

As a symbol of the social order, the freighter in Secret Tournament takes the place once occupied by Le Corbusier's ocean liner, for whom the ship was a symbol of progress. [Le Corbusier 1982, p. 75ff] For him, technology was the future, and Modernism's promise of redemption from industrial fabrication was found in its processual logic. The freighter in Secret Tournament is no symbol of progress, not a forecast of a better future, but instead its opposite: A dungeon, a prison, a space of life and death. The dream of Nike urbanism is not that of Modernism, not that of justice and equality, of social forms of collective life, but instead of the realization of the individual's private identity and its demarcation against others and against the attention of the many. Technical progress, the productive logic of industrialized society, is no longer the redeemer, but instead the enemy. With Nike, salvation is found elsewhere: In freestyle instead of on the conveyor belt; in experience, not in the (rational) division of labor. Postfordist hedonism has detached itself from Modernism's Fordist aspirations of universal prosperity. And if Le Corbusier's *Vers une architecture* is a call to arms ( i.e., the motto 'Architecture or Revolution'), then so too is the Nike spot. In Secret Tournament, the campaign emblematized by a scorpion logo, total competition prevails, and it is fast and deadly. Here, the difference between Nike urbanism and the grand Utopias of the past century becomes explicit. The ship no longer symbolizes the dream of progress, as with Le Corbusier, nor a heterotopic place of flight as with Foucault. It symbolizes not the dreams of Capitalism, but instead its reality: Only one of us can win, and it doesn't matter how.

During the 2000 European soccer championship, an old freighter was to Rotterdam what the former Stadion der Weltjugend was to Berlin. It lay in the harbor before the city as a Nike experiential space. Is it the future of the city to be the remix of an advertising spot? The brand makes the space available in which our social relations are mirrored. With Nike, this is the image of the combative city, of a remorseless battlefield of identity. This city reproduces and elucidates our competitive society. Only as an explanatory model can this advertising-become-space reach its target group. When that which the space narrates, scenarizes, renders experienceable, is also representative of that which inwardly moves consumers of this space. In the future experience-oriented city, the brand is a crucial agent, if not the paramount one. In that city, the brand becomes a partner in all forms of planning, the determinant of developmental trends. Precisely to the degree that economic decisions replace political ones, the brand displaces the primacy of the political in the shaping of the city. Niketown is not called that simply because it is a department store for sporting goods, but instead because Nike claims to transform the city it inhabits into a Nike city. Just as the Russian space station Mir was constructed as an instrument for the conquest of outer space, the Niketowns are the points of departure for the conquest of the city, for the generation of an imaginary Nike world. What the Mir is to outer space, Niketown is to the city: Welcome to Niketown.

# THE NIKETOWNS ARE CONSTRUCTED FOR THE CONQUEST OF THE CITY AS THE MIR WAS FOR THE CONQUEST OF OUTER SPACE.

# JUST DO IT –
# BRANDING, EXPERIENCE, IDENTITY

**BRAND PHILOSOPHY:** In 1988, Nike launched the slogan "Just do it", which has remained its central message to this day, the core value of Nike as a brand. In "Just do it", one of the best known advertising slogans worldwide, the entire spectrum of Nike's brand identity finds expression. Just as Niketown represents the ideal of a free, sportive city, the slogan "Just do it" is an appeal to a new self-image, to the Nike way of life. It stands for a break with everyday existence, for the freedom to do what you want.[9] Just do it, the spirit of Nike, means fighting and winning, even when that seems impossible.

On the meaning of the slogan, Nike states: "The Just Do It ad – it became both universal and intensely personal. It spoke of sports. It invited dreams. It was a call to action, a refusal to listen to excuses and a license to be eccentric, courageous and exceptional. It was Nike. This campaign (...) became part of America's history." [www.nike.com] Accordingly, the heroes of Nike are not only athletes like Michael Jordan, who push against the limits of the physically possible in his sport, but also ones like Cathy Freeman, who overcome social barriers through athletic performance. But in the sense intended by Just do it, Nike's pantheon of heroes consists not exclusively of successful star athletes, but also includes, for example, a wheelchair user and an 80 years old man who goes jogging every day despite his advanced age. [Goldman/Papson 1998, p. 3 and p. 20] To live according to the spirit of Nike means to reach the realm lying beyond your own limits. And Just do it means that everyone is capable of achieving this. Just do it asserts that we must free ourselves from our self-imposed shackles. The regimented city, then, is the point of reference from which we must disengage ourselves. That is why a New York spot from the mid-1990s shows André Agassi and Pete Sampras playing tennis on 5th Avenue. The mode of functioning of the city is thereby abrogated, the logic of the everyday ruptured. The street becomes a tennis court, the sidewalks stands. Agassi (the ingenious 'enfant terrible') and Pete Sampras (the consummate athlete), embody our dreams of escaping the mundane. Sports – in contrast to the everyday urban context – is scenarized here as an act of liberation. "Just do it." Or, as in the campaign for the opening of Niketown Berlin in 1999: "There are more ball courts than you think. One of them is right under this poster."

Sports as the liberation from the everyday and as resistance to the everyday constitutes Nike's brand identity, now fused with the popular cult of the body. Just do it means the incessant improvement of the self, emancipation from one's ordinariness, permanent performance enhancement. Just do it is the experience of victory in a struggle with one's own self and against all others. Just do it is no mere advertising slogan, but instead the motto of a competitive lifestyle. It has become a philosophy.

**WHAT IS NIKE?:** Is Nike a religion, an ideology or a political movement? Nike proffers a cult, a lifestyle, a basic attitude through which we can attune the maxims guiding our behavior. Nike speaks of revolution and propagates the image of another, better world. More than a mere manufacturer of sports articles, Nike sells more than shoes and sweatshirts. Nike is a proposal for experiencing my own self the way I would like to.

Like all movements, Nike has a leader. The difference between leaders and prophets (and hence also between movements and religions) is that while prophets speak of a fictive afterlife lying beyond the mundane world, leaders attempt to guide us toward an idealized here-and-now. Michael Jordan is no prophet of basketball playing who proclaims how one could play the game. Instead, he is, in reality, 'His Airness.' And Cathy Freeman really is fast. These are our heroes, and we want to follow them. They show us by example how we ought to live. Are they, then, the leaders of a movement? The maxim of this movement is Just do it, and worldwide, an entire generation has grown up with the slogan. This generation has internalized the rules of our society: Whoever fights, can achieve anything. It doesn't matter where you come from, it only matters what you can do. The Nike movement is a consummate blend of two primordially American virtues: The ethos of the immigrant, who starts out as a dishwasher and ends up a millionaire, and the Protestant-Calvinist notion that God's love can be gauged according to one's own prosperity and success, that striving brings us closer to Him. These two perceptions constitute the core of the contemporary American ideal, that of free competition that is embodied in Nike: Just do it, believe in yourself, be better than anyone else. We might conclude from these considerations that Nike is a fictive movement within the logic of consumer-oriented Capitalism. Nike transcends the basic rules of our society: In a society based on the principle of competition, each of us is compelled, in all circumstances, to try to reach our optimal physical and mental conditions in order to be capable of continued competition. I improve myself. I become myself: Fit for total competitive struggle. In this sense, Just do it can be interpreted as an ideological statement of totalizing Capitalism. At the same time, Nike stands for the precise opposite, for Nike generates the spirit of resistance, of the Guerillero: "I adhere to no laws, I do only that which I have set as my own goal. I am unrelenting toward myself, and I am the same with the world at large."

Nike is a brand, and it wants to sell products. To this end, it offers possibilities for identification. These offerings mirror the fundamentally contradictory nature of society, which is why we can identify so strongly with Nike, why Nike is such a successful brand. Simultaneously, Nike propagates the basic principles of Hypercapitalism (total self-exploitation and perpetual self-perfection), and resistance against the system (i.e., against regimentation, ordinariness, everyday existence, boredom and orderliness). Life becomes resistance and struggle. In the ideal of the experience Guerillero, the combatant, who fights simultaneously pro and contra himself, Nike amalgamates protest against Capitalism with the basic laws of capitalist self-exploitation. Nike anticipates resistance even before it emerges. And Nike is quicker than any protest movement – in the end, even antiglobalization activists have to wear sneakers. Nike reacts to fundamental social problems, thematizing contemporary grievances and problem areas (ranging from the city's functionality to the problems of disadvantaged youth) in advertising campaigns and urban interventions. At the same time, Nike makes available a 'philosophy' that serves as a model for

problem solving, while showcasing individual paragons who successfully live out this recommended lifestyle.

Nike's influence on everyday culture, on the development of moral
values and models of living, is comparable to the influence enjoyed by
political or religious movements. But Nike is no religion, no ideology,
not a movement. Nike is a brand.

AND NIKE IS Q

ANY PROTEST

IN THE END, E

GLOBALIZATIO

HAVE TO WEA

UICKER THAN
MOVEMENT
VEN ANTI-
ON ACTIVISTS
R SNEAKERS.

**LIFE AS EXPERIENCE:** Simulation is reality. Reality is simulation. The experience is the moment when we perceive ourselves as an 'I,' when we experience our individuality, our singularity, our being. I experience, therefore I am. The search for experiences has become one of our most crucial activities, to an extent our everyday labor. At the center stands the process of individualization and hence the questions: 'Who am I?' and 'What do I want to become?' The question 'Who am I?' is equated with the questions 'What have I experienced?' And the question: 'What do I want to become?' with: 'What can I anticipate experiencing in the future?' An essential displacement has occurred in the process of individualization, i.e. the salient attribute of modern societies. "In the old paradigm, the world was a given to which I had to adapt myself. In the new paradigm, this relationship has been reversed; if anything at all is still regarded as being given, then it the ego. (...) From a world-oriented subject to a subject-oriented world: this is the cultural-historical caesura occurring in the second half of the 20th century." [Schulze 2000b, p. 3] This caesura is so consequential that in comparison to preceding phases of the development of Modernity, contemporary society could be described as an experiential society. The distinguishing trait of this 'experiential society' is that the experience of one's self becomes the content of one's own life. "Inner-oriented conceptions of life, which situate the subject at the center of thought and behavior, have superseded outwardly oriented conceptions of life. Typical of members of our culture is the project of leading a beautiful life." [Schulze 2000a, p. 35] In the search for happiness and for a 'beautiful life,' new rational criteria are developed for making decisions, criteria that can be reduced to the formula: 'What have I experienced?' In the process, the individual becomes his own creator, his own 'experience manager,' is compelled to become inventive. "Individualization shifts the potential for self-fashioning, the individual action, to the center. (...) The shaping of the given biography becomes the task of the individual, becomes a project." [Beck 2001, p. 29] But this process is by no means a simple one, and not everyone is capable of rising to its demands. [Cf. Sennett 1998] The "demands of individual self-realization have in the meantime (...) become an institutionalized pattern of expectations vis-à-vis social reproduction to such a degree that they have sacrificed their inner purpose (...). The result of this paradoxical reversal (...) is the emergence of a multiplicity of individual symptoms of inner emptiness, feelings of being dispensable, aimlessness." [Honneth 2002, p. 146] The individual, who has become his own experience manager, is himself responsible for success or failure in the quest for happiness. [Cf. Müller-Schneider 2000, p. 25f]

The identity of the individual in the sense of the romantic ideal of authenticity is superseded by multiple identities that are tested experimentally, whether sequentially or parallel to one another. Identity, and the experience of one's own individuality, become consumer products. Everyday shopping becomes an activity through which the various facets of the ego may be tested and displayed. For Koolhaas, therefore, shopping is "the last remaining form of public activity." [Koolhaas 2001, p. 125] "Life has increasingly become a space for role playing and the mimicking of life styles" [Leach 2003, p. 5], and the city is one of the stages upon which we can live out this life.

Precisely this stage function is fulfilled by Nike's urban interventions, in which the city is converted into a double stage: A stage for a brand that represents a brand image, and a stage for the target group, which can practice a different manner of using the city. One may adopt a critical attitude toward this form of urban use, because, as Opaschowski characterizes it, such experiential worlds are "substantially artificial worlds, and did not evolve historically." [Opaschowski 2000a, p. 17] Such spaces can also be understood as dream spaces in which the paucity of experience in reality can be compensated. [Cf. Hasse 1994] "In consumption, we create new magical realms and realities, ones more beautiful, more spacious, cleaner, more exciting, and more authentic that their real world counterparts." [Steinecke 2000, p. 93] At least in the USA, consumption-oriented experiential spaces have become everyday spaces, and they represent an ideal version of reality – in the form of the mega-mall, the shopping center has not only become a substitute city center and rendezvous point, but even an amusement or theme park[10]. In the final analysis, it matters little whether we interpret the search for exceptional experiences as a compensatory attempt to escape a disenchanted, alienated daily life; as a positive expansion of the individual's experiential horizon; or as a logical transformation of Fordist industrial society into a late Capitalist service economy. To comprehend how these urban, experiential brand spaces function, it is far more relevant to see how alongside constructions of identity based on references to external elements and shaped via affirmative consumption and the recombination of preformed fragments of identity, there also exist inneroriented modes of self-perception. Via active participation in experiential offerings, these supply additional and crucial components of identity definition. Subground Battle is not just a strategic intervention in the urban realm, but also, from the perspective of the user, a singular, special space of possibilities where facets of one's own identity can be lived out in concert with likeminded individuals. For the self-actualizing, self-experiencing individual exists under constant pressure to succeed; hence the attraction of experiential offerings and promises. Precisely at this point, experience-oriented branding commences: While brands are abstract, pictographically transmitted identificatory proposals, the experiential brand space opens up completely new possibilities for identification. Here, consumers can discover new identities, contexts, and realms of feeling in the experiences on offer. The experiential space replaces the hero as a figure of identification; Niketown displaces Michael Jordan. In place of the projection of an ideal image steps an experiential space where a brand identity is communicated via new experiences. The construction of identity no longer emerges from the recombination of references to external, product-specific codes, but instead through an experience that is furnished with an identificatory offering. The consumer's attention is no longer directed toward a hero, because he himself becomes one. Experience-oriented branding combines the strategies of consumer-oriented identity construction with the parallel requirement for experience as confirmation, as positive feedback of one's own self-constructed identity. Experiential brand spaces become all-encompassing bids for identity determination: Brand + experience = identity.

**FLEXIBLE IDENTITY:** In 2003, a Germany-wide Nike campaign was called 'Show your Moves,' and was dedicated to the theme of 'Freestyle.' Young people from all over Germany were invited to show their best moves in soccer, basketball and break-dancing. A black Unimog toured through Germany's largest cities and filmed teenagers performing. The best players, who survived the final elimination, were invited to Berlin or Dortmund. Freestyle is the sporting equivalent of pretensions to social individualization. Freestyle means to develop one's own performance style, to exhibit sleights of hand and tricks with the ball, mixing dance and acrobatics in a way only remotely reminiscent (aside from the presence of a ball) of the original sport involved. Performances are accompanied by music, and one of the principal difficulties of Freestyle is to adapt the movements and tricks you have worked out and extensively rehearsed to the rhythm of the music, producing a flowing movement. Substituted for countable units such as goals, baskets, or points is the principle of entertainment value, the number of astonishing moments, the interest of the performance. Consequently, the 'Show your Moves' campaign was a collaboration between Nike and MTV, and the prize reward was not cash, but instead the prospect of appearing in an MTV video. The generally binding rules are replaced by Freestyle, whose legitimation is derived from the degree to which it commands attention and admiration. [Cf. Franck 1998] While the Bolzplatz campaign and the street soccer movement demanded a playful, creative approach to play (one that had already become detached from the rules of club sports), Freestyle takes individualization a step further. In place of teams, we find the individual fighter: There is no longer even an opponent. The sole adversary in Freestyle is the player's expectations of his own capacities: The degree of perfection.

Adorno had already characterized sport as a training instrument for the social struggle for survival: "Fitness for labor (...) is probably the secret purpose of sports. Often, we perform in sports first, enjoying it as triumph of our own freedom, that which is really performed under social pressure, and which we are compelled to render palatable to ourselves." [Adorno 1969, p. 65] Freestyle, then, reflects the double demand of our society to be highly individual while at the same time behaving flexibly within pre-given framing conditions – represented in Freestyle by music. [Cf. Sennett 1998] Hence, Freestyle corresponds more closely to social realities than team sports, which are based on interactions between players.

But even classical team sports like soccer display these social framing conditions in its development. [Lootsma 2002, p. 47ff] While until the 1980s, soccer was still strongly marked by the ideal of midfield strategists (the key player), today every player must be deployable in every position. The ideal soccer player is interchangeable, flexible. The striker has to defend, and the defense has to be able to go on the offense. Simultaneously, he must be an individual, a distinct personality, a star, in possession of special abilities. No other soccer player shows this as clearly as David Beckham. As a public figure, he is no longer a soccer player, but simply a pop star, a fact that became obvious when it was announced in summer of 2003 that he was switching from Manchester United to Real Madrid. The process of generating stars does not arise from the exigencies of the game itself, but from the technical necessities of marketing. The explanations offered for why Real Madrid bought David Beckham out of his ongoing contract with Manchester United make it clear that it was not a question of filling Luis Figo's position,[11] but instead of using him (he is very popular in Asia) to open up new merchandising and endorsements markets for Real Madrid. [Cf. Haupt 2003] Here, almost paradoxically, we find the requirements for personal exchangeability paired with claims to individuality and distinctiveness.[12]

With the Nike iD shoe, such notions of exchangeable individuality are converted into a product. On a Nike website [http://nikeid.nike. com], you can assemble an individualized shoe model from various colors and textures. The highpoint of this individualized shoe is the personal signature, a word composed of up to eight characters. Just like a genuine sports star, you can wear your name on your shoes. What appears at first glance to be the individualization of their products is revealed upon closer examination as pseudo-individualization within a pre-established system. Only a restricted selection of elements is available, although their combination is meant to yield a unique product. As in every process of standardization, the result has already been predetermined during the specification of methods and input elements; standardization always occurs in relation to options that have been set in place by the system. In order to offer the greatest possible range, the codes deployed by the system cannot be excessively complicated, a factor that further diminishes variety. "Brand name culture – Nike culture – gains its very strength through its superficiality. Through its surface affect, it seduces and offers itself up as an emblem with which everyone can identify." [Leach 2000] Moreover, this system incorporates far more essential limitations: Nike reserves the right to refuse signatures that fail to conform to their brand image. Such limits were highlighted by Jonah Peretti in 2001, when he attempted to personalize his shoes with the anti-globalization/anti-Nike slogan "Sweatshop," a request that was declined. [Cf. Peretti 2001]

Bids for identity circulate within a clearly delimited field. In this connection, identity and individuality mean neither authenticity nor uniqueness, but instead a form, just as within our society, the available codes communicate both affiliation as well as exclusion. But such preformed bids for identity can also be conceived as offering opportunities for escape, as standardized and flexible individuality becomes a sheet anchor in relationship to the ubiquitous pressure for individualization: "The retreat of the self into the non-self, the desired liberation from the compulsion to lead a unique, originary life." [Beck 2001, p. 30] "Almost everywhere, the dismantling of rigid behavioral norms leads not simply toward the formation of a new personality ideal, but instead only augments opportunities to appropriate cultural traditions on a broader basis which had previously been reserved only for certain minorities. Only secondarily does this process compel the development of altered patterns of identity." [Honneth 2002, p. 149]

It is not a question, then, of liberation, nor of new forms of personal expression, nor of a new ideal of the human personality. It is instead a question of a flexible identity, one that is and must be capable of altering according to the given situation in the course of the experiment called life, and which must have recourse to a pool of bids for identity, and to the corresponding urban experiential spaces.

# FREESTYLE IS SLAVERY OF SELF-PERFECTION

# SWOOSHTIKA RULEZ –
# RESISTANCE, CAMOUFLAGE AND
# COLLABORATION

**THE TRICKSTER:** Shopping is culture, and the consumer is an artist. While shopping, during the everyday acquisition of commodities, the consumer invents himself: Who am I, who do I want to be today? The construction of identity and communication proceeds via the deployment of codes that sponsor identity, codes with which certain styles, brands and products are invested. Identification and exclusion, transformation and affirmation. Shopping is the construction of identity and the scenarization of self-images. By collaging and recoding various product attributes, styles emerge that embody attitudes toward and views of life. The consumer is the protagonist who shapes his own self-image. But in this process, the identities developed by brand strategists and advertising agencies are not adopted unaltered by consumers. Rather, they are extracted, recoded, and collaged into a larger context of identity. The consumer, then, is refractory, following his own paths, acting creatively. This independent mode of reception extends from adaptation to reflection, and all the way to resistance. Consumption becomes a creative act, which is intrinsically productive: "The counterpart to rationalized, expansive (...) and spectacular production is another production, one referred to as consumption. It is cunning and dispersed, and it diffuses itself everywhere, soundlessly and almost invisibly, for it expresses itself not through its own production, but instead through its handling of products that are imposed by the dominant economic order." [De Certeau 1988, p. 13] Constructions of identity, then, by no means proceed as linearly as might seem desirable from the perspective of market strategists. For "Individuals are perfectly capable of existing reflexively and flexibly within more-or-less plural collective identities, together with their symbolism, and often capable of relating to these in a playful manner." [Bohrmann 2001, p. 99] Perhaps it is necessary to imagine the consumer as a kind of artist, one whose productivity is not based upon creating objects, but instead on the assigning of meanings. For that is precisely what the creative consumer does: He attributes meanings to things. In doing so, he has recourse to the brand identities that constitute an available repertoire of symbols; these are signs within a language spoken by the productive consumer. The creative consumer collages his identity together from snippets of pre-given bids for identity. And this collaging does not stop at the boundaries of his own body. You can brand yourself with a tattooed Swoosh, a continuous reminder to live out the philosophy of Just do it. In tattooing brands on one's own body, you display visually a felt inner connection to the brand image: I don't need to buy it, I just label myself.

The consumer as artist, the artist as consumer: Here is the formidable opponent of the marketing specialists. He attempts to transform the pre-given codes and images of branding, to defamiliarize them, to exploit them for his own purposes. For the technique of bricolage, the brand and its identity are regarded as raw materials, an operational guide in the jungle of offerings, a playing ball in the production of new meanings. [Cf. Liebl 2002] Here, we find a perpetual interplay between subcultural trendsetters and brand strategists. While the latter attempt to channel and control meanings that become invested in the brands they represent (and this is the real objective of product advertising), subcultures constantly endow products with novel codes, developing styles which, in turn, can be converted by marketing strategists into new brand identities that are compatible with the mainstream. What emerges is an eternal antagonism between the creative consumer and the brand strategist, a spiral without any terminus: Two avant-gardes, two guerilla groups dancing with one another in a circle, like a snake that bites its own tail...

From this perspective, the consumer is no longer regarded as the mere victim of his own 'false needs' [Marcuse 1994], but instead as a 'trickster' [De Certeau 1988] who maneuvers within a pre-established system, bringing about a new image of communicable identity. Identity is now transformational, undermining pre-given perceptual schemas and recreating itself. It is the result of a creative, inventive act.

**CAMOUFLAGE:** Global enterprises are dependent upon the effective transmission of brand experiences. For only in the context of individual experience can a brand be subjectivized by consumers, that is to say, successfully internalized. That is why marketing strategists seek to circumvent the trickster and his cultural techniques. With camouflage strategies, they increasingly attempt to annul distinctions between advertising campaigns and real life, and to integrate themselves into the existing bids for experience and identification while avoiding allowing the brand to make an aggressive appearance.

All of the interventions described up to this point are scenarizations of urban space. Even if individual experience is authentic, every user of such an intervention remains conscious of the fact that he is inside of a scenarized space, even if – as in the case, for example, of the Bolzplatz campaign – the borderline between staged and genuine activations of urban space becomes blurred. When such forms of intervention are heightened, the results are interventions that are no longer recognizable as brand specific scenarizations, and whose brand strategic background is disguised, or camouflaged. Such camouflage attempts to manage and to manipulate street credibility; they are covert operations launched inside the subcultural milieus of the respective target groups. In comparison to the interventions in the urban realm or in the familiar corporate theme parks, as described above, camouflage opens up new dimensions of branding. It attempts to endow the brand with the appearance of a self-evident component of the cultural codes current within the respective scene. Such cultural camouflage hoodwinks the trickster, seeking to penetrate into his unconscious, to instrumentalize his delight in play for other purposes.

"Get the people cooler than you" [cf. Rumack 2001] is one motto of contemporary marketing. Target group-oriented marketing attempts to win over opinion leaders of a target group which, it is hoped, will then follow of its own accord. [Cf. Frank 1998] Even Adidas' success in the American market (during the fitness and jogging surge of the mid-1980s, they lost their market share almost completely to Nike and Reebok) can be traced back to the recruitment of a group of opinion leaders. In the early 1980s, younger black hip hoppers turned away from over-branded companies like Puma and Nike, instead buying shoes and clothes from Adidas, a brand less advertised in the USA. Without Adidas having done anything to make it happen (or precisely because of the fact), their sneakers suddenly began to appear in music videos and to receive mention in song lyrics (*My Adidas*, Run-DMC 1984), becoming an instrument of differentiation: Adidas was now 'cool.'[13] [Cf. Bieber 2000, p. 149ff] In order to retain street credibility in the USA, and, by this, to reconquer shares in coolness lost to its competitors, Nike deliberately avoided prosecuting shoplifters and sellers of cheap counterfeits, a tactic that allowed members of black youth subculture (which had taken over the socio-cultural function of an opinion leader in the USA since the hip hop and rap surges) to acquire Nike clothing. [Cf. Klein Naomi 2001, p. 90f] Sales of Nike products on the American market are dependent upon prosperous, white suburban kids seeing 'cool,' black youth in Nike outfits – even if they were stolen.

The Berlin campaigns described above were also designed to gain street credibility for Nike, which is a long-term process. As explained by the head of the agency Aimaq Rapp Stolle, which conceived and implemented the various Berlin Nike campaigns: "At the moment, we are paying into an image account. (...) They [i.e., the youthful target groups: author's note] should be growing up with Nike." [Stolle, cited in Mohr 1999] Even the thematizing in Nike's advertising of problem areas such as Aids, the disadvantaged status of youth in inner city neighborhoods, or environmental issues serves to occupy areas of concern to target groups. [Cf. Goldman/Papson 1998, p. 172]

Camouflage reverses classical advertising strategies. Instead of branding an opinion leader, camouflage seeks to penetrate undetected into the home territory of the opinion leader, to insert itself within the opinion leaders themselves as a reference in their personalized identity collage. Cultural camouflage is an undercover action in which the manufacturer appears not as an agency of control or as a sponsor, but instead as a component of the source codes of a given scene. Cultural camouflage is an attempt to hijack the source code of the target group, to manipulate the mechanisms determining in/out. Brand strategists attempt to hack the subculture.

In cultural camouflage, the brand is valorized to the degree that it surfaces as a reference of scene-specific collages of individuality (among other references already accepted in the eyes of the target group). They affect the status of an already accepted code: It is a question of faked credibility.[14] The following examples are not perfect cultural camouflages, which may be due to the fact that the strategy used in a given cultural camouflage may be underdeveloped or poorly conceived. Or that I, as a part of the infiltrated system and a member of the target group, have failed to recognize an instance of cultural camouflage that is, in reality, flawless.

PRESTO, BERLIN 2001: Presto is the name of a Nike product line launched in Europe in 2001. Presto was, indeed, also the name of a club in Berlin that opened for a few weeks in summer 2001. It belonged to the tradition of Berlin clubs in the 1990s, spaces used only temporarily, and continually surfacing in different locations, each of them known only within a specific scene. Presto was located on Rosenthaler Straße, at the center of Berlin's nightlife district, and depended in both design and program on the tradition of illegal, temporary Berlin bars. Presto was a typical Berlin scene mixture, part club, part bar, part art gallery, with drinks and DJ, and more standing around than dancing (in the wake of the crossovers of the 1990s, Berlin had established a mixed form combining these three types). In appearance, the Presto Lounge seemed like a normal club. "Late in the evenings, it is difficult to find the place, so successfully has it assimilated itself to its surroundings (...). On the ceiling hangs a disco sphere, with collapsible rice paper lamps in front of the windows, some of which don't work. Toward the back of the space is a small bar. The walls are roughly painted in white, and contrasting with them is a slightly sinuous black stripe that runs across two walls at eye level. Along the stripe are mounted small plexiglas cabinets. Inside of them are (...) Nike sneakers." [Becker 2001] In contrast to the Bolzplatz campaigns, in which public space was to have been conquered for a youth target group, the Presto Lounge was addressed to the Berlin clubber. In keeping with the logic of cultural camouflage, it was to remain undetected that the bar was initiated by the agency

Schubert und Schubert on a commission from Nike. The Presto Lounge was intended to make the impression of like other clubs that sprang from the scene. The sneakers — the actual motive for the lounge — pose in this context as more-or-less inconspicuous decorative elements. It is precisely via their inconspicuousness, via the implicitness of the presentation, that the strategy of cultural camouflage becomes effective. It should remain unnoticed that the bar is a form of advertising, since the objective is to have the shoes become an element in the coding of a club that blends into the scene: Presto has arrived in Berlin Mitte. A year later, additional temporary Presto Lounges were set up in modified form in Munich, Cologne, Hamburg, etc.

In Canada, the Presto product line was introduced in 2002. Just as in Berlin, Nike attempted to gain a foothold in the subcultural scene by opening a temporary gallery, the 'Presto Space of Art,' in Kensington, Toronto's artists' and scene quarter. As in Berlin, the gallery was also a club. Decisive for this campaign were the results of a study on 'instant' street credibility that Nike had commissioned from Youthographic, a youth marketing agency from Vancouver. [Cf. Hardie 2002] In the Presto space, artists could exhibit their works without restrictions – only the display of other brand logos was forbidden. [Cf. Rumack 2002] Differently than in Berlin, there was protest in Toronto once it became known that the gallery was an element of Nike's marketing concept. The resistance movement Opresto (a play on the word 'oppressed') was established, and they organized a protest concert, the 'Art Space' that was strewn with multicolored bags. Presto was closed again after a few weeks, because resistance against infiltration in subcultural milieus was too strong.

# "DON'T LET YOURSELF BE EXPLOITED BY YOUR CITY EXPLOIT YOUR CITY"

Text on a poster for the opening of Niketown Berlin in 1999

**SPIRITROOM, BERLIN 2002:** Berlin's Spiritroom is a kind of showroom, and has occupied a former retail shop in Berlin Mitte, in the immediate vicinity of galleries and bars, since 2002. The space is run by an advertising and PR agency based in Berlin and Hamburg. Spiritroom is a space designed for presenting the new Nike collection. The products are addressed to the 'urban consumer' who favors comfortable, sports-oriented, yet fashionable clothing. To date, two Nike collections have been featured. In order to establish greater credibility among the members of the target group, younger designer labels such as Anne Schmuhl and ADD were displayed in the Spiritroom alongside the Nike collection. In the eyes of the target group, Nike (or the commissioned agency) is not simply financing an expensive showroom. Instead, someone from the fashion industry is combining recent, trendy designer fashions with interesting products from mass-marketed labels like Nike. To approach this in the spirit of crossover (collages of items not really belonging together, for example, Prada and H&M, whereby the orientation is toward designers, not labels), is the strategy of this cultural camouflage. The space is redecorated for each collection. For the first collection (spring/summer 2002), the young Berlin designer group Pfadfinderei Mitte was hired, while designer Chris Rehberger/ double standard was engaged for the fall/winter collection 2002/2003. [Streetwear Today 4/2002] Spiritroom is not publicly accessible, but is only opened on special occasions. The target groups are brokers from the media sector, who are invited to special Spiritroom events.

But the camouflage strategies exploited by marketing experts are not confined to the cultural spheres of target groups, but instead attempt to intervene in the larger social fabric. Corporate citizenship is the watchword under which enterprises become socially engaged in the Anglo-Saxon tradition that entails acknowledging social responsibilities, while focusing in the process on their most important locations. The corporation, according to this tradition, feels responsible for alleviating social problems and returns a portion of its profits to society in order to assist socially underprivileged individuals. "Global companies too must be active locally, embedding themselves in the public sphere." [Dittmann 202, p. 32] Worldwide, Nike sponsors hundreds of different social and ecological projects, most of them based locally and hence able to certify concrete successes, on the basis of which the positive commitment of Nike as a global player can be communicated. [Cf. www.nike.com] A special type of this form of public involvement is employee volunteering. Berlin's Niketown goes to Kreuzberg: Volunteers from Niketown Berlin offer young immigrants and foreigners instruction in basketball, volleyball and soccer, including a concluding tournament. [Cf. UPJ-Service-büro 2003] The youth to be reached come from socially weaker districts like Kreuzberg and Lichtenberg, and belong to groups of socially under-privileged youth. Nike conceives this action as an expression of the company's consciousness of its social responsibilities. Not only does the corporation actively provide financial resources; it also releases its staff from work to spend a few hours a week training young people (i.e., they are paid for engaging in these activities). In Berlin Nike collaborates with various public agencies specializing in youth and social work.[15]

The classical arguments favoring corporate exploitation of such public engagement emphasizes the positive image transfer achieved in a given location. In the long-term, every corporation profits from the local cultivation of a positive image, whether by recruiting employees, or through public decision making processes in whose context a good image can have positive implications. The promotion of non-profit activities on the part of employees, referred to as 'employee volunteering,' also improves worker motivation and strengthens identification with the employer. Employee engagement becomes an effective tool of personnel development. But beyond such easily conceivable benefits of non-profit volunteer activity, others are readily evident, especially concerning strategies described as camouflage, ones that might even prove to be the most essential. An employee may become a contact person for the target group. In Berlin, after all, Nike employees do not work in retirement homes, but instead with young people. In doing so, they are able to pick up surreptitiously the codes, dialects, and ways of thinking of target groups. And the function assumed in the USA by black youth culture is occupied in Germany by foreign youth groups oriented to the black youth culture of the US. This strategy is doubly useful: Employees can convey a positive image and cultivate personal relationships with youth who serve as opinion leaders within their social milieus. Young people thereby become multipliers. At the same time, employees get to know the target group and in the process gain greater competence in the context of sales talk with customers.

The camouflages described here penetrate into the source codes of the subculture of the target group. In the process, the boundary between artificial marketing- strategies and the everyday world of the target group vanishes. Remaining for a moment with the image of a source code, we can say that camouflage marketing behaves like a virus that manipulates and influences the script of the source code. Now marketing abandons the realm of advertising, of fiction, of the promise that can never attain fulfillment, in order to breach reality itself, even to create new realities.

**BRAND HACKING AND BRAND SABOTAGE:** What forms of protest or resistance against the various marketing strategies remain possible if marketing itself masks itself and behaves like a guerillero? Can brands be sabotaged? An additional development of the techniques of the trickster is brand hacking, which goes beyond the creative reception and recoding of brand images. By hacking, we mean a cultural technique for infiltrating existing systems, either to investigate them (analytical-empirical approach), or to identify vulnerabilities or potential points of attack (subversive approach). The concept became familiar as a term from the programming scene. Today, hacking is a generalized cultural technique which attempts to decode systems and penetrate them in a transformative way. [Cf. Liebl/Ullrich 2002, p. 29] Hacking, then, is a subversive act. People engage in hacking for a variety of reasons: simply for the fun of it; to demonstrate their abilities and skills within a specific scene; to highlight gaps in a system; or as a form of critique.

Various approaches to brand hacking are found in the contemporary arts. Many artists who deal with the everyday phenomena of consumer culture are preoccupied with the presence of brand-specific bids for identity and with their contemporary forms of reception. There is Sylvie Fleury with her fetish objects, Danielle Buetti with his branding photo-montages, and Olaf Nicolai with his inflatable sneakers, to mention only a few examples of works that attempt to document the social significance of brands by using the strategies of contemporary art. But the critical impulse is not always understood as such. New York artist Pascal Spengemann works with sneakers, which he provides with the labels of other brands. While he conceives of his work as a form of critique [Weiner 2003], dealers want to acquire his shoes as objects to be offered for sale, because they regard such cross labeling as expressions of the attitude of the collagists of identity. In contrast, in the late 1990s the Berlin group 'Chicks on Speed' sold manufactured sneakers in order to intervene subversively in the economic cycle of commodities. "Adidas are going to give us these shoes (…). We're going to resell them as 'ModifiedAs'. We're going to take off the stripes, punch holes in them…" [Beware 2000] Brand hacking becomes especially interesting once it leaves its initial habitat in galleries and museums to begin sabotaging the functioning of brands in everyday spaces.

An example of brand hacking in a public space could be observed on a Berlin basketball court. Berlin Alexanderplatz, 1994: As a contribution to environmental protection, Nike initiated a worldwide program involving the use of recycled sneaker soles to pave ball courts. Under the title 'I was an AIR Jordan,' "the first public recycled basketball court in the world" came into being, according to Nike's advertising. [Cf. Woznicki 2002] In contrast to the fictive conversion of 5th Avenue into a tennis court in a filmed advertisement starring Agassi and Sampras, the basketball court at Alex is real. Alexanderplatz is surrounded by GDR-era prefab concrete high-rise slabs. This once prestigious consumer landscape, now slated for demolition, is a forlorn residual zone, an emblem of a lost Utopia of progress and civility. Today, Berlin Alexanderplatz numbers among the so-called dangerous locales, with its drug dealers, punks and high police presence. For Nike's concept of improving the world through sports, Alexanderplatz is an ideal background, where the charm of the rundown concrete towers and multilane streets present a hostile urban environment within which a basketball court can become a gem of the game, of Just do it philosophy.

It was precisely such an instrumentalization of space that the artist Marc Bijl attempted to undermine when, in autumn of 2002, he installed a cast concrete Swoosh in the basketball court. Following its removal, he replaced all Nike logos and texts in the park and on the baskets with the Adidas logo. A Nike court was thus metamorphized into an Adidas court. Significantly, Nike Berlin's first reaction was to contact the agency representing Adidas in order to find out whether Adidas was responsible for this guerilla action. While this was not the case, the Adidas agency would not be deprived of an opportunity to poster the re-branded court with ads for the Adidas City Games, a replica of Nike's urban interventions. In the meantime, all logos – both those of Nike and of Adidas – have been painted over in black. Out of a brand space, a logo-free zone has now emerged. To whom does urban space belong? Adidas? Nike? The users?[16]

**VIENNA, EARLY AUTUMN 2003:** On Karlsplatz stands a Nike container informing the public that in early 2004, the square surrounding St. Karl's Church is to be renamed 'Nike-Platz,' and that a 36 meter long Swoosh sculpture will be set up there. The project is presented comprehensively and by means of a flawless Nike aesthetic on an Internet page that bears the title 'Nikeground – Re-Thinking Space.'[17] According to the web page, the names of central squares in 13 cities worldwide would soon cease to commemorate dead kings and generals and instead bear the Nike name. A citizen's movement mounted an opposition to this scandalous proclamation. A few days after the container was set up, Nike made it clear no such Nike campaign existed, while the city of Vienna categorically denied that negotiations involving Nike and the renaming of Karlsplatz had ever taken place. Soon, both the container and the 'citizen's initiative' were revealed to have been a critical dramatization staged by Public Netbase, a Vienna media arts platform, and the Italian artist's group 0100101110101101.org, a media fake that seeks to call attention to the progressive economical rationalization of all spheres of life.

The protest forms of brand sabotage and brand hacking are characterized by their high resonance in the media, and they contribute to awakening public awareness of certain problems. Nonetheless, they suffer from a drawback: Structurally, they are defensive, and they remain affirmative despite their antagonistic stance. In order to be effective within an economy of attention, such actions must of necessity be subordinated to precisely the same marketing logic they attempt to criticize. For this reason, they proffer no positive alternatives, no counter-model to the imperatives of the compulsion to sell.

With brand hacking, the boundaries between art, critique and participation disappear. Is the fictive company Ingold airlines [www.ingoldairlines.com] a critique of the service Zeitgeist or a blueprint for the perfect airlines? And isn't Ora-Ito's hack-Mac [www.ora-ito.com] conceivable as an Apple product for hipsters? The creative potential of the hacker becomes a tool of brand policies: "Without exception, hacking and its associated phase of disorientation offers opportunities for intro-ducing improved or novel bids for orientation in the brand context." [Liebl/Ullrich 2002, p. 29] Critiques of the system are taken up and exploited in order to test resistances to disturbances, hence strengthening the system – no differently from the way the software industry hires hackers to test security systems developed by the industry.

COLLABORATION: The marketing strategy of adapting forms of expression drawn from protest culture represents a problem for those who want to resist the hijacking and transformation of public space by Nike and other corporations: Their protests come to nothing, because the language of the protests has already been hijacked by their opponents. The kids who use the basketball court at Alex simply do not care who finances it. The consumer as artist, the artist as hacker: Both are sources of inspiration for brand strategists who derive stimula-tion from critiques and transform them into novel strategies. Brand strategists not only hack into subcultural realms, they even go a step further by attempting to get artists and activists onto their side. Adidas hired brand hacker Ora-Ito as a product designer, and Nike also attempts to recruit artists from the street art movement as campaign designers.[18] But the protagonists of the local subcultures themselves also establish contacts with marketing bureaus, offering their services as collaborators in creating camouflage strategies, thereby profiting from the financial possibilities and medial presence of the brands.

The story of Berlin's WBM Bar clarifies how brands and subcultural actors profit from one another, how they enter into covert pacts involving cash payments in exchange for credibility in eyes of target groups. The leitmotif of the first WBM Bar, which existed for a few weeks in summer of 2002 in Berlin-Mitte, was that of the apartment. WBM stands for 'Wohnungsbaugesellschaft Mitte' (Housing Development Corporation), a local institution that began offering affordable apartments for rent in Mitte beginning in the 1990s. The WBM Bar was only open to friends of the owner, and entry was gained via a red key, 300 copies of which were distributed within the scene for the opening.[19] In the tradition of illegal Berlin clubs, the bar was only open on certain days of the week. It was decorated in a neo-pop 70s style, like an apartment, with armchairs, sofa, and a coffee table. The walls were papered with large-format photographs that narrated a story of a pretty girl who spends the day in Berlin-Mitte. At first glance, no camouflage strategy was in evidence. But upon closer examination, it became obvious that every motif bears an item of Nike apparel, and that here and there lies a Nike soccer ball. Everywhere, in fact, discreetly yet perceptibly, the Swoosh logo surfaces. This is cultural camouflage: The Swoosh gains access to a fashionably styled club milieu, where it is to be accepted by the (previously selected) clientele – and moreover a clientele whose members function as opinion leaders – as a self-evident element of the constructed atmosphere. What came first? The idea of a bar for friends, for which an innovative camouflage concept for product placement was developed for the sake of winning Nike as a sponsor or financing partner? Or did the bar have its origins in the recognition that within the club scene, promotional measures can only succeed if they are conceived with extreme subtlety? In the idea of a Nike club that would avoid detection within the scene, passing instead as a cool' underground club? In contrast to the Presto Lounge, the WBM Bar was, in fact, illegal, for it was located in a typical apartment building, from which it was evicted after two months because of noise disturbances. In its subsequent location, no Nike insignia were to be seen, whether because of negative feedback received from numerous visitors whose suspicions had been alerted by the presence of so many Nike logos. Or else because (as claimed by both of the Bar's initiators) after the success of the first WBM Bar, no external subsidies were required for the realization of their design concept.

Not just Nike, but Adidas too works with strategies of cultural disguise, attempting to counterfeit authenticity. In 2001 the first Adidas Original Store opened in Berlin, a concept store for a new line of products, the Adidas Originals. In the meantime, there are now two additional Original Stores, located in Tokyo and New York. The Adidas Originals are aimed at a target group that no longer engages intensively in athletics, but which nonetheless cultivates a sporty lifestyle and wears classical sportswear in combination with other designer labels, whether at work or in the evening in clubs. The Adidas Original Store is located in Berlin-Mitte in the immediate vicinity of scene specific fashion boutiques. Parallel to the opening of the Adidas Original Store, Adidas began to implement marketing strategies in Berlin that resemble those of Nike. Events include hip hop concerts in the Original Store, a 'roof basketball' tournament on the roof of an old building in Friedrichshain, and a 'pool soccer' tournament in a disused indoor swimming pool in Mitte, all staged under the motto: 'Your City - Your Arena.' While Nike focuses on individuality through competitive distinction and perfection, Adidas inaugurates a new type of bid for identity: Individuality through being different, through eccentric individuality. Under the motto 'Once Innovative, Now Classic, Always Authentic,' Adidas distinguishes itself from Nike's competitive self-image. In 2003, for the new season of the Adidas City Games, the readership of the Berlin city magazine 030 was invited to submit ideas for new types of sports and their suitable locations, which can then be realized in collaboration with Adidas.

As a partner in the first implementation of these urban interventions, Adidas recruited the Turbogolfers, a group of men ranging in age from their late 20s to early 30s. The Turbogolfers see themselves as a riot group that occupies urban spaces for golfing, thereby subversively undermining the codes of distinction governing golfing. To be sure, the Turbogolfers use genuine golfing equipment, including bags and the various clubs, and they play according to the rules of the Royal and Ancient Golf Club of St. Andrews (aside from their own, constantly newly-defined playing rules). But they play not on golf courses, but

THE SUBCUI
TRANSFORI
OUT OF THE (
CULTURE EM
ACQUIESCEI
AVANT-GAR
TO DO THE B
GLOBAL MAI

TURE
IS ITSELF:
OUNTER
E RGES THE
IT STYLE
DE WAITING
IDDING OF
KETING.

instead on military premises or construction sites. Moreover, the ball is not teed into holes; instead, the goal is redefined on each occasion: An abandoned car, an inflatable paddling pool, a windowpane, an air-raid shelter... Meanwhile, the Turbogolfers are just as proud of their beer consumption as they are of such inherently illegal uses of spaces. [Cf. Wenderoth 2002] As with the creators of the WBM Bar, this form of collaboration is based on mutual interests: The Turbogolfers would like to see their distinctiveness, their delimitation from the banality of normal city users mirrored according to the laws of a medial society. [Cf. Franck 1998] Their collaboration with Adidas, then, supplies confirmation that they are indeed something out of the ordinary. In return, Adidas is accorded credibility with the 30+ target group, because they are able to emblazon themselves with protagonists of successful individualization, with cutting edge, authentic everyday heroes of unconventionality.

On the basis of the approaches examined above, we might describe the marketing strategists as urban actors who intervene actively and covertly in the design and use of urban space. The brand becomes a partner of the consumer, helping him to experience and to scenarize himself while shaping the city (Your City – Your Arena). In the process of individualization, the brand sponsors the presentation and testing of one's own self-created identity. Simultaneously, the creative consumer becomes the concealed partner of the brand, an agent who collaborates with the brand and procures admission to target groups. The trickster has changed sides to become a collaborator, a willing handmaiden of global marketing. Metropolises like Berlin or London have evolved into colossal laboratories for lifestyles and trends of daily living, into experimental fields for trendsetters and trend researchers, to be cultivated conjointly by subcultures and marketing bureaus. The subculture transforms itself: Out of the counterculture emerges the acquiescent style avant-garde waiting to do the bidding of global marketing.[20]

# CORPORATE SITUATIONISM –
# THE LAST UTOPIA AND ITS FAKE

Nike's urbanism shows similarities both with drastic urban critiques as well as with the emphatic model of a "different city for a different life" advocated by the Situationists, the artist's group once gathered around Guy Debord. What brings us close to the Situationists today is the radical critique of the rationalism of modernity and of social alienation, as well as the resultant demand for a new kind of urban development, for a different way of perceiving the city, of reading and using it. On this point, intriguing parallels are detectable with the critique of the city given expression in Nike's campaigns. Such comparisons fail to do justice to the artistic and political motifs of the Situationists, who radically opposed Capitalism. [Cf. Debord 1996, p. 10] Meanwhile, the imaginary Niketown is born of Capitalism itself, is an apotheosis of the Capitalist city. This comparison does not attempt to reappraise the content or the intentions of the Situationist movement, but instead to broaden the discourse about Nike's urban interventions. For if we apply a Situationist template to Nike's urban interventions, we arrive at a problematic that goes to the heart of Niketown and its model of the city as a brand specific experiential space: Is Niketown the affirmative fulfillment – now transformed into commercialized form – of the vision of a Situationist city: is this 'Corporate Situationism'?

**ANOTHER CITY FOR ANOTHER LIFE:** At the center of the Situationist movement stands a confrontation with the city as the experiential sphere of everyday life. "The urbanism of the Situationists was directed against an obsolete and impoverished functionalism, and proclaimed the testing of the city as a laboratory for the playful revolutionizing of everyday life. Planning and building were to have been nothing less than the realization of a philosophy, a collective Gesamtkunstwerk." [Costa 1998, p. 74] The Situationist city was to have generation of chance events and by the incessant transformation and reversal of hegemonic relations. Accordingly, they wanted to supplant functionalist zoning with a city of play and adventure: "We demand adventure. Some people are searching for it on the moon, since they can no longer find in on Earth. First and foremost, we are always committed to a transformation on this planet. We intend to create situations – new situations. We take account of the rupture of the laws that inhibit the development of effective activities in life and in culture. We stand at the threshold of a new age, and already today we are seeking to conceptualize an image of a happy life and a unitary urbanism – an urbanism for pleasure." [Constant, 'Another City for Another Life,' cited in Wigley 1998] The ideal of the Situationists was urban situations, "constructions of a different kind, which should lead toward radically new forms of life." [Levin 1998, p. 70] This city is characterized by the emergence of fortuitous events, move-ments, continuous change. "One day, we will build cities for wandering." [Debord, 'Theorie des Derivé,' cited in Levin 1998, p. 75] The city of the future, as imagined by the Situationists, is a city of experiences, of dis-covery, of rebellions against the compulsions of a regimented life. "Every street, every animated square, could be the entrance to a metropolis, a prelude to a discovery through which life opens up, through which new faces are perceptible, with habits shed and familial duties or regulated professional lives now regarded as marginal epiphenomena, by which a free movement no longer cares to be disturbed." [Ivan Chtcheglov (Gilles Ivan), 'Formular für einen neuen Urbanismus,' in I.S. NR 1, cited in Ohrt 1990, p. 50] The architect of this city is no longer the designer of individual buildings, he is the creator of processes and atmospheres that allow room for the unfolding of individual freedom.

The analysis of the real-existing city as a functionalist, inhumane space, and the dream of a free city as counterproject: Here are the inter-sections between historical Situationism and Nike's urban, experiential brand spaces. The imaginary Niketown, as the scenarization or simulation of a better reality, responds with exactitude to the drawbacks of the con-temporary city as analyzed by the Situationists: The absence of the magical, the unknown, the unforeseeable. The urban brand spaces, then, emerge within voids of meaning torn open by the functionalism of con-temporary urbanism, which subdivides the city in functional terms while seeking to extirpate everything wicked, abysmal, dark. The fantastic city, the dreaming city, the different city, that of desire and of secrets, has vanished, sanitized in the process of modernization, and divided into residence, living, working. Today, we are confronted by an emotionless, aseptic city, whose sole alternative, apparently, is the artificial experiential space. The newly emerging brand worlds, hence, are also characterized as places of re-enchantment [Sellmann/Isenberg 2000] to which a spiritual surplus may be attributed, [Bolz 2003] in the sense that they accommodate moments of the spiritual, of the non-logically deducible, within the disenchanted world of Modernity. Or, as Situationist Gilles Ivan has characterized the task of a future urbanism: "A rational expansion of the old religious systems, the old fairy tales, and especially psychoanalysis, becomes more urgent every day, to the degree that passion increasingly vanishes. Everyone will, so to speak, occupy his own cathedral. There will be spaces that permit better dreaming than drugs; houses in which one can only love (…) The quarters of this city could correspond to the catalog of the various feelings encountered accidentally in normal course of living." [Ivan Chtcheglov (Gilles Ivan), 'Formular für einen neuen Urbanismus,' in I.S. NR 1, cited in Levin 1998, p. 71] Would not such a city be the dream of any urban marketing?

DETOURNEMENT AND FAKES AS MARKETING ILLUSIONS: As one of their methods for bringing a Situationist city into being, Debord and Wolman developed the strategy of détournement, of reversal and misappropriation. Détournement relates both to objects and to spaces, to actions as well as to methods of perception. The core of détournement is to tear an object from its original context and to situate it in a new one, but in such a way that it still refers to its original context, with this multiple referentiality making new modes of reading possible. Détournement takes place when someone, to use a famous example, wanders through the Harz Mountains carrying a city map of London. "All elements, no matter what their sources, can become objects of new contexts." [Debord/Wolman, 'Gebrauchsanweisung für Zweckentfremdung,' 1956, cited in Levin 1998, p. 73] The strategy of détournement can be understood, then, as a means of communication that serves, through reversal and irritation, to convey critical new contents and to subtly enable novel

THE POSSIBILI

PLORATION IN A

NIKETOWN AR

MORE THAN A F

CONSTRUCTED

TIES FOR ▮▮-
A FUTURE
NOTHING
AINSTAKINGLY
FAKE

experiences. Subterfuge and irritation are essential functional mechanisms. Out of the strategy of détournement, developed in the 1970s, evolved the fun and communication guerilla [cf. Blisset/Brünzels 1998, p. 65ff], who made the fake an important element of action-oriented media and social critique. "A successful fake plays with the classifications of author and text. Its effectiveness unfolds precisely where it permits no unambiguous references to emerge: At this moment, the meanings of the affected statement begin to oscillate, and new interpretations become evident and available. With the fake, the principle of interpretative variability, which acts in conventional processes of communication as an unavoidable disturbance factor, is the foundation that makes the fake's mode of communication possible in the first place. The fake wants not to be taken literally, but instead to trigger reflections about the originator and the content of the message." [Blisset/Brünzels 1998, p. 67]

The Situationist strategy of the fake and of détournement can be discovered as an instrument of communication in nearly all of Nike's urban interventions. They serve here the same function as they do with the Situationists and media guerillas, namely to gain access to new spaces of interpretation and opportunities for reflection. But with Nike, the brand stands in the foreground, not the political statement. The signs on the Bolzplätze, with their interdictions ('Enter at your own risk'; 'No bottles') are intended to trigger exactly the same mechanisms in the target group which Blisset/Brünzels have described as the effects of the fake. This strategy is found in multiple forms in Nike's campaigns, whether on posters ("There are more ball courts than you think. One of them is right under this poster." Niketown opening, 1999), or in Happening style actions. As when a group of young artists (accompanied by the requisite media) stormed Berlin museums to install posters reading "Down with the Spanish champions." Here, the soliciting of public attention follows the pattern set by the media guerilla, and observers may well have believed these were in fact young artists attempting to come to terms with the musealization of art. But the group storming the museum were actually paid actors hired by an agency to install advertisements for a soccer match between the club Hertha BSC Berlin, sponsored by Nike, and FC Barcelona – the Spanish (soccer) champion.

Nike has deployed the strategy of the fake at its most consequential in Australia. In the Berlin campaigns exploiting this strategy, target groups were always aware that they were dealing with advertising. Every young person who heard a Nikepark 2000 radio spot, intercut into another advertisement in the style of a pirate broadcast, knew he was listening to Nike's own promotion, but still found the spot 'cool' because it mimicked an illegal action by a media guerilla. With the radio spots for the Bolzplatz campaign of 1999, which faked genuine contributions to the 'Fuck You' hotline on Kiss Fm, a Berlin radio station, the listener had to realize, at the latest upon hearing them repeated, that this was an ad campaign. The implementation of the strategy of faking takes on another dimension in campaigns that actually try to operate like communications guerillas. In Australia in summer of 2001, Nike launched a new soccer shoe, Nike Air Zoom. On posters that imitated the aesthetic of the protest movements, especially the Billboard Liberation Front, which is very active in Australia, the shoes were referred to as "The Most Offensive Boots we Ever Made." These imitations were so skilful that even within the anti Nike scene, there was controversy about which elements came from Nike and which from its opponents. Yet Nike's faking strategy extended much further: The campaign organized a protest group, the FFF (Fans for Fairer Football), that protested against the technical superiority of the new Nike soccer shoes. The highpoint of the campaign was a series of demonstrations held in various Australian cities to protest the superiority of Nike sport shoes. Yet these demonstrators were not genuine: "They were not activists (...) these were 'actorvists'." [Rebensdorf 2001b] In the tradition of media-critical fakes, Nike destroys the symbolism of its political enemies by adapting their communicative means and subversively undermining these. In this case, Nike faked an entire anti-Nike campaign, including demonstrations and anti-Nike web pages.

There are good reasons for supposing that Nike's marketing strategists have devoted serious study to the artistic and political protest movements of the previous century. Critically depressed, Debord wrote in 1988 that of the readership of his Society of the Spectacle, "half of them, or nearly that many, are people who are committed to maintaining the system of spectacular authority." [Debord 1996, p. 193] Marketing strategists deploy the instruments of the protesters, not as a means of critique, but instead in order to construct a brand image of resistance.

But comparisons between the Situationists and Nike marketing strategists can be extended even further: Are Nike's urban interventions, and is not the situative brand city, not actually the fulfillment of the Situationist dream of an experientially intensive city – albeit not as a social, Utopian project, but instead as a consumable simulacrum? "The great coming civilization will construct situations and adventures. A science of life is possible. The adventurer is the one who allows adventures to happen, not so much the one to whom they happen. (...) The share of those little accidents we call fate will be reduced. For this goal, an architecture, an urbanism and an influential form of plastic expression coincide, of which we possess the initial foundations." [Debord, Wolman et. al. (Internationale Lettristen) 1954, cited in Ohrt 1990, p. 79] Target group specific market research, trend research, brandscaping, scenarizations of atmospheres: Are these not truly the "science of life"?

When Nike converts a subway tunnel into a pipe for skateboarders, when basketball and soccer is played in it, when for just a moment, the legality of the rational city is suspended, a détournement has taken place. And if it is staged not in a subway station, but instead under the Reichstag (which is, after all, the seat of legislative power), then Nike pinpoints ways of using the city that come undeniably close to those of the Situationists. But there remains an enormous and unbridgeable difference. While the Situationists were striving for freedom, for excess, then brand specific Corporate Situationism pursues a reliable, controllable, consumable image of freedom. Nike follows not the project of a libertarian way of life, but instead a marketing illusion. [Cf. Ada Louise Huxtable, p. 90ff] The possibilities for exploration in a future Niketown are nothing more than a painstakingly constructed fake.

# LEARNING FROM NIKETOWN –
# THE BRAND CITY
# AND ITS DREAM MASTERS

What does Niketown imply for our understanding of the city? For the practise of architects and planners? Is Nike's urbanism – as a form of Corporate Situationism – the prototype of the future city? Must we learn from Niketown? Or should we instead – in the face of novel global social challenges – reinvent the task of architecture in order to proffer a successor to Modernism? And in the face of Nike's sophisticated urbanist strategies, what possibilities for intervention are available to those who adopt a critical stand toward the brand city, and who understand architecture and planning as social projects?

**FROM THE THEME PARK TO THE BRAND CITY:** The leitmotif of urban planning over the past 15 years has been the theme park. The city, as an object of consumerist desire, as an ensemble of products aimed at certain market segments and contingents, becomes itself a more-or-less successful brand. As such, cities are subtended by the same principles of marketing and scenarization as other brands. The brand city communicates both outside and within as a singular family of products, namely lifestyles, cultural offerings, life qualities, landscapes, architectures, languages, gastronomy, etc. The city itself becomes a consumable product. Symptomatic of this development is the competition for the title of most attractive global city in the Pacific region, whose leading contenders are Hong Kong, Sydney and Shanghai. Olympic Games, Disney Parks, and ambitious architectural schemes are the building blocks used to construct a city's image, which seek to synthesize touristic qualities such as entertainment, recreation and culture with local various economic, cultural and political features. [Murphy/Watson 1997, p. 37ff and Sassen 2000] Using the example of Manhattan in the early 20th century, Rem Koolhaas [cf. Koolhaas 1994, p. 29ff] has shown how the theme park is a role model for the construction of the modern metropolis. Today, Las Vegas – a theme park that itself consists of numerous different theme parks – is the emblem of the artificial city, containing nothing genuine. Here, everything seen by visitors is fake, and the result is a kind of consumerist Fata Morgana. From a European perspective, Las Vegas is a Disneyland become city (Disney's Celebration is too small to yield a truly anxiety provoking symbol).

The theme park is the ruling paradigm for the construction of the marketable city: "Finally, this new realm is a city of simulations, (...) the city as a theme park. (...) The architecture of this city is almost purely semiotic (...). Such design is based on the same calculus as advertising, the idea of pure imageability (...)." [Sorkin 1992, p. XIV] Today, it is already observable how cities are reconfigured along their sightseeing tours, with each tourist attraction staged like a ride in a theme park, structured into a time/attention unit. As in every theme park, new rides are regularly installed (Millennium Dome, Leipziger Platz) and routinely updated. Theme cities like Berlin offer every facet of contemporary entertainment, just as it is found in theme parks: From the Ghost Ride, inspired by the horror genre (the Holocaust Memorial[21]), to futuristic visions (the Sony Center); from the glories of history (Brandenburg Gate, Royal Palace, Pariser Platz), to the idealized present of the main street (Potsdamer Platz, the Daimler-Chrysler complex).

The theme park, then, has long since arrived into the reality of the city – in fact, the contemporary city is a theme park. Within the development of marketable urban images and postcard pictures, architecture assumes an important, even central role, and architects are the set designers of this scenarization of the city. Against this background, the critique of the theme park (which seems to have become a generalized cultural asset, one cultivated by many architects) takes on the appearance of a pretext, a chimera, little more than a cheap distracting maneuver: "Disneyland is positioned as imaginary in order awaken the impression that everything else is still real. But Los Angeles, and the America that surrounds it, have already ceased to be real, they belong instead to the order of hyperreality and simulation. It is no longer a question of false representations of reality, but instead of disguising the fact that the real is no longer the real, thereby rescuing the reality principle." [Baudrillard 1978a, p. 25]

What triggers popular critiques of the theme park is perhaps fear of something else, something far surpassing the theme park itself, something that brings far more radical transformations of the city in its wake. Perhaps it is even the fear of Niketown. One could argue that the interventions discussed in this book are small-scale, temporary intrusions into the city, and that such incursions are unlikely to have any sustained impact on such vastly complex urban systems. But Niketown Berlin demonstrates the contrary. Measured against the investments involved, these interventions are both highly effective and extremely efficient in reaching their intended target groups. The small scale and temporary interventions of Nike urbanism assume the contours of a new city. At the center of this new understanding of the city stands variety, the continuous re-scenarization of the city that make experience possible, along with the spontaneous use of the city, the testing of identities. The interventions reviewed here are prototypes of a new way of deploying the city, in which constantly changing urban spaces are transformed into spaces for brand-specific identificatory experiences, into stages for the scenarizing of individuality.

For the brand city reaches more deeply into the mechanisms of the city than does the theme park. It is an optional film that is spread across the entire city, while the theme park is a fixed section, a tourism hot spot. Fear of Niketown, of the brand city, is more than fear of the city that is conceptualized along purely commercial lines, more than the fear that the city is becoming a staged leisure activity park, an artificial fantasy world. It is the fear of a creeping infiltration into all areas of life.

In the future, brands – as producers of bids for identity and as purveyors of experiential spaces – will be the most powerful players in the urban microstructure. Market strategists have discovered the valence of real spaces because in spatial experience, feelings of actuality and veracity can be generated: I experience, therefore I am. In the absence of the brand city, brand identity remains only an image, a picture, a hollow promise. In urban space, it becomes a proposal, an optional reality through which brand becomes experienceable. Associated with this is an essential transformation of urban space. Since brand experience is always a staging that necessarily negates, blocks out, dispels certain

BUT NIKE ADAPTS
OF CRISIS REACTI
COVERT OPERATIO
UNITS INTEGRATE
WOVEN NETWORK

# THE STRATEGIES
## N FORCES:
## NS, AND FLEXIBLE
## O INTO A TIGHTLY

aspects of reality, the staged space of the brand city must be controllable. In place of notions of a city under constant surveillance (in the Orwellian sense), we find the idea of a preformed experiential city, the city as a brand specific experiential space. Might Gilles Deleuze have described the dystopia of a city in the society of control any differently had he been acquainted with Niketown? [Deleuze 1993, p. 265]

The image of a future Niketown, an ideal brand city, is more than a picture of an urban theme park. It is the image of a controlled and staged city that remains – at least on the surface – exactly as it is today. In the USA of the mid-1950s, cinemas are said to have increased ice cream sales by inserting advertisements for ice cream, lasting only fractions of a second, into the evening's feature film. These advertising images were never consciously perceived by cinema audiences, but instead only subliminally (hence the premise of the method). In *The Hidden Persuaders*, Vance Packard describes this phenomenon as the 'Subthreshold Effect.' [Packard 1957, p. 41f] The examples of temporary interventions described above with reference to Nike correspond precisely to this tactic: The spatial continuum of the city is no more interrupted than is the narrative flow of the feature film, but the subliminal messages are received all the same. Similarly, minute interpolations into spatial experience make an impression on the unconscious.

While the theme park constructs a completely new stage setting, Nike urbanism spreads a new, temporary layer visibly across the entire city, which itself remains intact with all of its highlights and its infamy. Both the corporate theme park and the brand-specific intervention in the urban realm attempt to render the respective brand identity experienceable using spatial means, and to create a space for scenarizations that make possible the experience of brand identities. Corporate theme parks (for example the VW Autostadt in Wolfsburg, Germany) constitute independent worlds that are closed off to the outside as secluded, self-contained scenarizations. The visitor/consumer enters a corporate theme park and finds himself in another world where he can experience the brand. Urban, experiential brand spaces seek out urban residents and target groups. The city resident is primarily interested in visiting an experiential space, not a brand space. The simultaneous transmission of a brand identity, as calculated by market strategists, is merely a spin-off effect. Urban, experiential brand spaces, then, function with greater subtlety than corporate theme parks. As a transparent layer, an ephemeral coating, the brand city delineates an unlimited territory, while the corporate theme park always remains an island. The strategy of urban interventions which composes the brand city is more sustainable than the corporate theme park, because the intervention can occur anywhere and hence the brand identity can erupt at any location within the city. In comparison with the urban interventions of the brand city, both the city as theme park and the corporate theme park – although recent developments – already seem obsolescent, awkward. We might map out a hypothetical genealogy registering the development of the brand city, from the shop in the city to the flagship store that is independent of location; from the flagship store to the corporate theme park; and from the corporate theme park to the brand city. If the theme park configures a stage set, composing artificial worlds, then the brand city of urban interventions constitutes (even if only temporarily) a section of reality. With Nike urbanism, a fragment of reality takes the place of a parallel world.

The brand city is based upon a completely different strategy than those used previously in urban planning processes. It is comparable only to military strategies that have emerged with the globalization of military deployments and which are comprehensible as being representative of new cultural paradigms within a globalized world society. Operative in the brand city – in place of the static planning principles of classical urban planning and of theme and amusement parks – is the flexible concept of Nike's urban interventions. This Nike urbanism makes possible shorter reaction times and rapid tactical shifts. In its physical form, the brand city is materialized only temporarily, surfacing briefly only to vanish once again – while nonetheless becoming permanently inscribed, in the process, in the long-term memory of a given place. It creates nothing new, but instead manipulates the preexistent, intervening actively in communicative and identity forming processes, adapting the methods of the trickster, who recodes products and is hence productive. The productions of Nike urbanism are predominantly immaterial. They does not alter the built space, but instead alter our perceptions of it, of its histories, recollections, and meanings, reorganizing our mental map. The large-scale amusement and corporate theme parks attempt to mount impressive shows, like a conventional armed force with its massive contingent of tank battalions. But Nike's strategy involves the use of rapid response or crisis reaction forces: Covert operations, on a small scale, using cost-effective and flexible units capable of operating in a variety of theaters, and of functioning simultaneously independent of one another, while at the same time integrated into a tightly woven network. Just as a globalized military has evolved altered strategies in the era of post-national war (cf. among others Kittler/Kluge 2003), marketing strategists in an environment of global competition imitate the tactics of guerilla groups and special forces.

Niketown is synonymous with the new city, which responds flexibly and contextually, in its own economic interests, to the needs of the Postfordist individual and his search for happiness and experience, developing new urbanistic strategies for this purpose. For Niketown does not come into being primarily because Nike constructs new buildings, nor because it makes new infrastructures available, but instead when Nike reinterprets available infrastructures, imposing new models of valuation on preexistent spaces, and intervening manipulatively in the mental map of the respective target groups. Learning from Niketown means grasping the functional dynamics of the experience-intensive strategies of activation in the city of globalized capitalism. It also means bidding adieu to the planning paradigm of Modernism, means giving up the dream of creating a better society through planning. Just as Niketown offers the prospect of a new city, Nike urbanism provides us with the blueprint of a new functionalism.

THE DREAM MASTERS OF EXPERIENTIAL FUNCTIONALISM: In light of the emergence of the brand city and the methods of Nike urbanism, we are confronted, as architects and urban planners, by a fundamental paradigm shift. Space is longer at the center of our conceptual scheme, but instead the experiences made possible by space and the identities it conveys. The significance of unmediated design retreats behind that of the metalevel of communication and experience.

Space emerges not via its aesthetic-sensuous construction, but instead through its contentual supercharging, through the significance of the bids for identity inscribed in it. The development of communicative processes in space, the fashioning of meanings, of contentual assignments, stands increasingly in the foreground in relation to what is normally conceived as classical functional design. Do we find ourselves, then, in a situation similar to the one confronting the founding fathers of Modernism, who had architectural methods at their disposal that no longer offered solutions to fundamental social and economic conditions? "Each age must search for its answers (...). Our MoMo forefathers did so against the backdrop of totalitarianism, world war class system and the atomic bomb. We must do so against the backdrop of capitalist globalization (...). Nobody could say that our agenda is less important or demands a less concerted response than theirs." [John Allan 2002, p. 24] Classical Modernism inaugurated a new architecture and a new planning logic that reflected the prevailing economic and cultural conditions, and at the same time sought to lend expression to visions of a better life. Do we need a new concept of functionalism today in order to do justice to the demands posed by the present?

In a society that has transformed itself into an 'experience society,' and whose cities are (brand) experiential urban realms, architecture and urban planning are ostensibly faced with new tasks. They must facilitate high experiential quality, stimulate communication, convey (brand) identity, and should provide a consumable home territory. Out of sociocultural and economic transformations grows a new conception of functionalism: Experiential functionalism. Experiential functionalism strives for activation and bids for identification, for the development of multiple spaces of offering. In the experientially-intensive, activated city, the task of architects and planners will be, not to design three-dimensional images, but instead intensive experiences; to plan not fixed situations, but rather small-scale communicative processes. The planning of activation will be the most important task facing the future shaper of cities, because the socialization of the individual will take place within such activations. Urban space in the experientially functionalized city will be composed of various temporary actions and interventions, which will be spread out like a carpet across the existing urban framework, thus rendering it perpetually newly readable and experienceable. The experientially functional city is more flexible, temporary, and processual than our contemporary city; it will be a space for spontaneous activities as well as for consumable, determinate experiential scenarizations. Like the functionalism of classical Modernism, experiential functionalism will be determined by economic framing conditions, and will also respond to social tasks. But experiential functionalism faces problems different from those once confronting Modernist functionalism. It seeks answers to problems related to individualization and the search for identity, and is simultaneously confronted by strategies for its economic utilization.

Two interest groups will oppose one another in the future city. First, the globally operating enterprises, the new urban players who require other framing conditions for the production of space and new guideposts for the staging of brand experiences. And second, the (critical) users of this city who seek a city in accord with the everyday need for experience, a city that facilitates adventure, revelation and experience, one that is secure and consumable for some, yet free and heterotopic for others.

Classical Modernism, emblematized by the appeal "Vers une architecture," was always intimately bound up with a moralistic credo, with the hope that the reshaping of the living environment would lead to the creation of a new man, would give birth to a better society. What are the consequences of this for the self-image of the shapers of an experientially functionalized everyday world? What will be the attitude of the architects and planners of experiential functionalism toward such all-encompassing claims, which account for a substantial portion of the fascination exercised by Modernism?

For Klingmann, future architecture will be reduced to the production of consumable objects: "As a mediator between cultural and economic interests, architecture can no longer evade the spatial and temporal imperatives of market culture. In the framework of global competition, architectural and urban forms emerge under virtually the same conditions as do consumer commodities." [Klingmann 1999, p. 46] In the field of tension between user and global player, on the other hand, Norman Klein sees architects faced with an important cultural task: "The global civilization has begun to settle in. We see its monuments more clearly, its glitter, its brutality. Thus, we as critics, architects, urban specialists, can outline its features more inventively, more playfully. We have to humanize the furtive idiocy of it. (…) And yet, its possibilities are extraordinary. The next decade promise to be crucial. The challenges are breathtaking." [Klein, Norman 2001, p. 451]

What is to be the ethos of the future architect? Will he become the "whore" nominated by Philip Johnson as a role model for the architectural guild? Will he be a dream master of Corporate Situationism? Or is there an alternative? What perspective can the architect – the shaper of spaces for life in the future brand city – adopt? The Situationist ideal of the architect was that of the shaper of situations, processes and milieus which could offer spaces for the living out of individual freedom: "The architect (…) will henceforth be a builder not of single forms but of complete ambiences." [Constant 'Rapport inaugural de la Conférence de Munich' (1959), cited in Wigley 1998] The architect of the brand city, the mainstream paradise, is also the designer of realms of feeling and experience. Yet viewed realistically, he designs not free spaces in the Situationist sense, but brand-specific, regulated, spectacular interiors. The architect of the brand city can no longer mobilize the image of the social community that impelled the architects of classical Modernism, nor the dreams of freedom pursued by the Situationists. From this perspective, when the architect of the future takes a backward glance at his own past, the view can only be a cheerless one: The noble master builder has become a dream master who endows the bids for identity designed by marketing strategists with spatially and sensually experienceable form. He has adapted himself aggressively – while keeping an eye out for lucrative commissions – to the altered conditions and demands of reality, bid farewell to the moral and aesthetic rigorousness of Modernism, and devoted himself instead to the everyday practices of experiential consumerism. In the long run, even the contemporary and frequently adopted posture of withdrawal into an aesthetic and technological realm, which frees architects and planners (at least on the surface) from

the reproach of being collaborators, cannot spare them from this fundamental revision of their sphere of responsibilities. On the contrary, the
prostituted architect, delighted to receive any contracts, designs experientially functional spaces where brand adventures and situations
can be discovered and innocuously experienced. For the brand city
(whether Nike city or any other) is a controlled environment where the
disposition of each individual space is predetermined, where freedom
and choice are only simulated. The occupation and use of such spaces is
not spontaneous, but instead strategically planned. The result is not
situations, but instead scenarizations: A simulated rupturing of the
system, a simulacrum of resistance, a mere feint of simulation.

In contrast to the trickster-consumer à la Michel de Certeau, the
dream master is not vulnerable to the illusion that he enjoys any headstart in relation to his putative adversary. And the dream master, so
proud of his prostituted posture, knows all too well that the trickster's
headstart can only be of brief duration, that his presumed oppositional
cunning will simply be usurped for the sake of system-immanent
improvements. That is why the dream master does not see himself as a
practitioner of a social avant-garde, but instead as a trend researcher of
lifestyles who markets and spatially implements newly minted ones. As
part of a corporate avant-garde [cf. Bouw/Dean 2001], the dream master
represents little more than a funereal afterglow of the master builder of
Modernism, who dreamt of realizing a new and better world through his
designs. Such aspirations disintegrate in the harsh reality faced by the
dream master, who wants nothing more than to be a manipulator of
spaces. But what are the alternatives to adopting the role of the dream
master? And what methods, tactics, options for action are available to
individuals who seek alternatives?

COUNTER CAMOUFLAGE AND RADICAL OPPORTUNISM: The
architect who does not wish to function as a dream master of Corporate
Situationism must evolve perspectives transcending those of the brand
city, ones that nonetheless do justice to contemporary sociocultural
developments. Needed are experientially functional perspectives for a
city where performance and experience assume central roles in the

multiple constructions of identity, a city oriented toward self-presentation, self-experience and self-exploration, but one that is not staged, controlled, or predetermined. Even architects who critically oppose the brand city need to recognize the mechanisms of experiential functionalism as a given of contemporary reality, and integrate them into their methods, working approaches and objectives. It is a question of implanting a realm of possibilities in this reality of the future city, one that allows for activity, spontaneity and self-presentation going beyond purely profit-oriented marketing strategies. But which resources and strategies are available to critical architects and space tacticians once the forms of expression devised by the subversive avant-gardes have been appropriated by marketing experts and preempted by promotional campaigns – once (as in Australia) even the protest form of the demonstration has been simulated?

With the advent of experiential functionalism, we witness the passing not only of the concept of functionalism advocated by classical Modernism in the fields of architectural and spatial production, together with its moral-ethical impetus, but also the temporal horizon of planning. Spaces are no longer planned for the long term, for the future, but instead staged for the present. It is precisely at this point that the architect must interpose himself if he wants to be more than a space manipulator. He must take possession of the methods of branding and globalization, converting himself into a seasoned, reactive tactician. Only then can he explore possibilities within contemporary and future realities for creating spaces for events that have not been predetermined in advance. The ideal Modernist planning and of the Modernist credo "Vers une architecture" is now supplanted by spatial tactics and temporary interventions: toward a new spatial tactics.

In order to implement his goals, and unless he wants to end up an ineffectual trickster, it is recommended that the tactician of the spatial cultivate exorbitant unscrupulousness. [Cf. Borries/Boettger 2004] In order to master the methods of the marketing strategists, he must pursue a counter camouflage. In place of the subversive trickster who is out-witted by the camouflage strategies of marketing experts emerges the radical opportunist who opens up free spaces in the gaps of the system,

# „WE DON'T SELL DREAMS WE SELL SHOES."

Nike slogan from 1996

designing temporarily autonomous zones. In the reality of the brand city, strategic actions oriented toward long term goals are no longer possible, and attempts to construct Utopias for a better future have become futile. The tactician of the spatial must be capable of responding quickly in order to contend with the 'rapid response troops' of Nike urbanism. His only chance lies in reactive behavior, in the tactical maneuvering through which he can exploit suddenly and fortuitously breached spaces and definitional gaps. At the center of the space tactician's labors is not the search for aesthetic forms, but instead for novel tactics capable of deployment in space, ones allowing him to appropriate spaces. The space tactician is the contemporary answer to the guerillero. But he is not a fighter who withdraws into the primeval forest, inspired by ideological romanticism. Instead, he is a pragmatist creating interference in the zones lying between decision makers, acting adaptively as a double agent in the context of various events: Counter camouflage. Only as a radical opportunist, as a flexible architect without attitude who is capable of oscillating between market, avant-garde and critique, can he foster freedom. A spark of hope remains...

# EPILOGUE

All of us are aware that the 'hidden persuaders' continue to be ceaselessly active; everyone knows that the public sphere has been thoroughly commercialized. But evidently, there is more to the story. Commodities have burst from the restricted arena of the display window, the gallery and the department store, where they have accumulated to the point of mutual paralysis: Lately, the pleasures of consumption are being sold to us directly, with the commodity itself being disseminated as a kind of free bonus. Images of the city act as culturally established bearers of merchandising messages: Boutique streets, shopping malls and theme parks are all configured around consumer articles. The prefabricated house industry no longer markets prefabs, but instead client-oriented residential atmospheres set in super snobbish residential parks where the houses, enfolded in greenery, quicken the pulses of the prospective buyers' hesitant economy of desire. The car discovers its identity in the corporate theme park, where the sought-after feeling of intense bonding is elicited more effectively than in the most competent garage.

Friedrich von Borries sprints through the city in his sneakers, where sensitized in this way, he detects the hidden insignia of the sports and leisure wear industry in the most diverse locations – especially the swoosh logo. Left far behind by the observations assembled in *Who's Afraid of Niketown?* are both hitherto discussed scenarizations of the city and the pessimism (or euphoria) of previous diagnoses of commercialization. His analyses constitute a real event in the discourse on urbanism. The entrance of brands as urban actors is characterized by Borries as a kind of virus that penetrates into the source codes of youth culture. Nonetheless, he argues that youth culture is not exposed defenselessly to this influenza, as simplistic stimulus-response theories constantly warn. Very much to the contrary, the clientele ride the tiger in the sense that, as cunningly resourceful super players, they construct their multiple identities via changing brandcodes, only to discard, transmit, etc., these later on, almost like swing voters. Is this too a kind of Neoliberalism from below? At least now, the one-sided sender-receiver model is undermined, and a transactional system temporarily constructed, one that would reverse the actions of product manufacturers to view them as responses. Juxtaposed with this are the manifold reflexive strategies by which the brand name is marketed in the form of a vehement critique of its own products. That such spiraling configurations cannot function without causing tendential enhancement of use value is indeed the hope of the theory of the "productive consumer." Borries does not go so far as to assert that the present-day consumer actually dictates commodity production, nor that he shapes the atmosphere of the cultural environment – in other words, that he becomes a cultural producer. Such an optimistic bias would have impaired his capacity for observation. Especially when it is realized that we require additional investigations of the life cycles and of the currency of the lifestyles prevalent in various subcultural and social layers. Such investigations would provide a more detailed picture of the long-term effects of these phenomena on certain impoverished and underprivileged segments of the youthful population, those residing in slums and peripheral areas. Friedrich von Borries has written a highly readable, searching book, one that sets a valuable accent on the currently re-emerging discussion about urban participation.

Günther Uhlig

# NOTES

**1** A condition entailed by the well-known (Heisenbergian) Uncertainty Principle. **2** The interventions accompanying the campaigns of 1999 and 2000 were supervised by the agency Schröder und Schömbs, Berlin, and beginning in 2001 by the agency Schubert und Schubert, also of Berlin. See: http://www.s-plus-s.com/ **3** Kristina Hille, project coordinator with Schubert und Schubert, from an email of May 18, 2001. **4** The players come from all nations known for soccer enthusiasm, from Japan to South America, making the spot usable worldwide. **5** A year later, together with Zinedine Zidane, Carlos, Figo and Ronaldo made up (wearing jerseys by Adidas) the 'white ballet' of Real Madrid. In the 2003-2004 season, David Beckham also played for Real Madrid. **6** See also Koolhaas 2004. **7** There were and are Nikeparks in other European cities, for example in Paris (Champs Elysées and La Défense), London (Millenium Dome) and Rotterdam (the harbor). During the World Cup of 2002, there were 13 Nikeparks worldwide. Nikepark Berlin was visited by more than 60,000 young people. **8** The ad campaign for Berlin was developed by Aimaq Rapp Stoll of Berlin, and it received various awards from the German advertising industry. See: http://www.ars-berlin.com/ **9** The agency Wieden + Kennedy has supervised Nike for many years. See: http://www.wk.com **10** The American DIY (Do it yourself) movement of the 1990s can be understood in this connection as a reaction to Nike's Just do it. **11** Alongside the theme park, the shopping mall was the most important prototype for urban planning. The shopping mall becomes a place where the socialization of various groups occurs, and it becomes a rendezvous point in the evenings, a destination for family outings. [cf. Fiske 2000, p. 26ff and Miller, 1998 p. 14ff] Like the amusement park, the shopping mall has become a destination for tourists, and shopping becomes an aspect of vacations. The 50-hectare West Edmonton Mall, for example, contains an ice-skating palace, a large aquarium with dolphins, etc., an amusement park with roller coaster, and a hotel. Alongside these commercial offerings, the mall assumes the function of a community center and offers, for instance, dance classes for seniors. In Germany, on the other hand, the slogan "experiential shopping" has established itself, and the construction of cities has become oriented toward the functional style of the mall. [cf. Arbeitsgemeinschaft Stadt und Center 1999] **12** While the American mall is a kind of substitute for an absent town structure oriented toward a center, in Germany an urban concept has come to prevail that, unlike the mega mall, is composed of mini malls, referred to as Urban Entertainment Centers, along with pedestrian zones and cultural objects. [cf. Ronneberger/Lanz/Jahn 1999, p. 67ff] As we can easily observe at Potsdamer Platz in Berlin, the success and public acceptance of this type of urban space can be measured by the degree to which tourists (whether from the Berlin metropolitan area or from further away) frequent it for shopping purposes. **13** Luis Figo, Portuguese soccer player, plays like Beckham on the right outer position. **14** This displacement in soccer betrays similarities with the altered self-image of architects. [Cf. Lootsma 2002, p. 47ff] **15** A similar phenomenon has been observable for a few years with Puma. It remains to be seen whether Puma will succeed in establishing itself as a big player beyond the retro hype. **16** But camouflage can also go in the opposite direction: Gelbmusik, a Berlin DJ group, applied large yellow stickers bearing the word "gelb" (yellow) in New York subway stations. The stickers were also furnished with a Swoosh logo. One of the initiators explained: "the swoosh is (...) a camouflage for the text, so the stickers won't be removed as quickly..." The strategy of camouflage, then, is here reversed: An artist's group disguises itself as a global player that is apparently engaging in a sham subversive action. **17** Gangway, Grenzräume So 36, Agens 27. **18** According to information from the social workers of 'Gangway,' who supervise youth who play at Alex, this symbolic rebranding has encountered no resonance. **19** Cf. www.nikeground.com **20** Cf. Swoon/toyshop: "I want to be part of the city that I live in," in *arranca!* No. 28, winter 2003/2004. **21** On the basis of the founding of clubs in the Berlin club scene, club homes have been opening for some time in which a form of legalization of otherwise illegal clubs takes place. [Cf. Dobberke 2002] **22** I encountered the concept of Corporate Situationism in the intro-ductory text to an interview by Chrystian Woznicki with Tom Holert [Holert 2002], as an undocumented and unexplicated term. **23** References to the Holocaust Memorial, the Topography of Terror, or the Jewish Museum as a Ghost Ride, like the Tunnels of Horror found in theme parks, strikes us (with good reason) as impious. Yet in light of the specific background of the interminable Berlin discussions about the memorial, this excessive characterization has its justification. For in various public debates, the necessity for a central place of memory was disputed in an especially pointed way since, it was argued, the Topography of Terror (at the heart of Berlin) and the concen-tration camp in Oranienburg (not far from the German capital) are both authentic yet chronically underfunded memorials, both consequently in need of refurbishment and upgrades. The advocates of a central Holocaust memorial opposed this argument by stressing the prominence of the proposed site, arguing for the spatial integration of the flow of visitors facilitated by the proposed location of the memorial, especially in cases of official occasions such as state visits. Yet such arguments correspond precisely to the principles guiding the layout of the spatial configurations of theme parks. My comparison of the memorial with a theme park is meant in this connection, and points up its intended spatial proximity to the other 'rides' (Postdamer Platz, Brandenburg Gate).

# IMAGES

**Danielle Buetti,**
Courtesy Galerie Bernd Knauss, © VG Bildkunst

**Bolzplatz Campaign,**
Berlin 1999

**Brand Hacking,**
by Marc Bijl, Berlin 2002

**WBM-Bar,**
© WBM 2002

**Campaign for the Opening of Niketown,**
Berlin 1999, Photo: Krystian Woznicki

**Nike Berlin Vandale, Special Edition 2002,**
Photo: Marcel Meury

# LITERATURE

**ADC-**Buch (2002), Mainz, Verlag Hermann Schmidt, **Adidas** (1997), Presseinfo 'Adidas AG plant neue internationale Hauptverwaltung in Herzogenaurach', Adidas AG, **Adidas** (2002), Annual Report 2001, Adidas AG, **Adorno**, Theodor W. (1969), *Stichworte/Kritische Modelle 2*, Frankfurt a. M., Suhrkamp, **Allan**, John (2002), 'A Change of Values', in: Henket, Hubert-Jan/Heynen, Hilde (ed.), *Back from Utopia. The Challenge of the Modern Movement*, Rotterdam, 010 Publishers, **Allard**, Marie (2002), 'Oubliez Nike, pensez Presto', in: *La Presse* 29.07.2002, Quebec (http://www.cyberpresse.ca/reseau/tendances/0207/ten_102070122269.html), **Andersen**, Neil (2002), 'New Feminism, Postering & Democracy, Corporate Sponsorship of Artists (a 1/2 hour Questionaire)', in: *Much News Looks At #1*, (www.chumlimited.com/mediaed/guidepage_much.asp?studyID=114), **Angélil**, Marc (2000), 'Urbane Kartographie', in: Neitzke, Peter/Steckeweh, Carl/Wustlich, Reinhart (ed.), *Centrum – Jahrbuch für Architektur und Stadt*, Basel/Boston/Berlin, Birkhäuser, **Arbeitsgemeinschaft** Stadt und Center 'Erklärung von Leipzig', Bau, **ARS**, Werbeagentur Aimaq Rapp Stolle, www.aimaqrappstolle.de, **Augé**, Marc (1994), *Orte und Nicht-Orte*, Frankfurt a. M., Fischer, **Baudrillard**, Jean (1978a), *Agonie des Realen*, Berlin, Merve, **Baudrillard**, Jean (1978b), *Kool Killer*, Berlin, Merve, **Beck**, Ulrich (2001), 'Individualisierung, Globalisierung und Politik', in: *Arch+* 158, **Becker**, Stephan (2001), 'Presto Lounge – Der schnelle Aufenthaltsraum', in: *Scheinschlag* 8/2001, Berlin, **Beware**, Cocoa (2000), 'These Monsters I can feel', in: *AMP*, August 2000, von: www.sci.fi/~phinn-web/links/artists/CoS/media/amp.html, **Bieber**, Christoph (2000), *Sneaker-Story*, Frankfurt a. M., Fischer Taschenbuch-Verlag, **Binder**, Reinhard (2002), 'Neue Chancen oder das Ende der Kreativität', in: *Architektur für Marken*, Dokumentation des 1. Fachkongresses 'Corporate Architecture', Rat für Formgebung, Frankfurt a. M., **Bittner**, Regina (2001), 'Die Stadt als Event', in: Bittner, Regina (ed.), *Die Stadt als Event*, Frankfurt a. M./New York, Campus, **Blisset**, Luther/Brünzels, Sonja (1998), *Handbuch der Kommunikationsguerilla*, Hamburg/Berlin/ Göttingen, Verlag Libertäre Assoziation, Schwarze Risse und Rote Straße, **Blumenstein**, Gottfried (2002), 'Carmen unter der Käseglocke', in: www.mdr.de/kultur/buehne/274945-hintergrund-397304.html, **BMW** (2002), *BMW Erlebnis- und Auslieferungszentrum*, Ausstellungskatalog Galerie Aedes, Berlin, **Böhme**, Gernot (2001), 'Zur Kritik der ästhetischen Ökonomie', in: *Zeitschrift für kritische Theorie* 12/2001, **Bohrmann**, Regina (2001), 'Urbane Erlebnisräume als Zonen des Liminoiden', in: Bittner, Regina (ed.), *Die Stadt als Event*, Frankfurt a. M./New York, Campus, **Bolz**, Norbert (2000), 'Kultmarketing'', in: Isenberg,

Wolfgang/Sellmann, Matthias (ed.), *Konsum als Religion*, Mönchengladbach, B. Kühlen, **Bolz**, Norbert (2003), 'Der spirituelle Mehrwert der Marke', Vortrag auf Werbekongress 2003, Berlin, www.werbekongress.de, **Borries**, Friedrich von (2000), 'Résistance', in: *Archithese* 4/00, Zürich, Niggli, **Borries**, Friedrich von/Böttger, Matthias (2004), 'Jenseits von On/Off', in: *Arch+* 169/170, **Bowlby**, Rachel (1993), *Shopping with Freud*, London, Routledge, **Bouw**, Matthijs/Dean, Penelope (2001), 'Corporate Avant-Garde', *Werk, Bauen + Wohnen*, Oktober 2001, **Britton**, Donald (1996), 'The Dark Side of Disneyland', in: Welt, Bernard, *Mythomania*, Los Angeles, Art Issues Press, **Certeau**, Michel de (1988), *Die Kunst des Handelns*, Berlin, Merve, **Costa**, Xavier (1998), 'Le grand jeu à venir: Situationistischer Städtebau', in: *Daidalos* 67, Berlin, Gordon & Breach, **Crawford**, Margaret (1999), 'The Architect and the Mall', in: *You are here*, London, Phaidon **Daimler-Chrysler** (2002), *Architektenwettbewerb Neues Mercedes-Benz Museum*, Ausstellungskatalog Daimler-Chrysler, Stuttgart, **Davis**, Mike (1992), *City of Quartz*, New York, Random House, **Debord**, Guy (1996), *Die Gesellschaft des Spektakels*, Berlin, Edition Tiamat, **Deleuze**, Gilles (1993), *Unterhandlungen*, Frankfurt a. M., Suhrkamp, **Dittmann**, Christoph (2002), 'Marke und öffentlicher Raum', in: *Anlage 1/Architektur für Marken*, Rat für Formgebung, Frankfurt a. M., **Dobberke**, Enno (2002), 'Vereinsmeierei en vogue', in: www.telepolis.de/deutsch/inhalt/co/13016/1.html, **Drilo**, Coco (2001), 'Das RAF-Mode-Phantom', http://www.salon-rouge.de/raf-hype2.htm, **Eberle**, Ute/Stöbener, Dorothée (2001), 'Gutes tun mit Gewinn', in: *Die Zeit* 39/2000, **Fainstein**, Susan S./ Gladstone, David (1999), 'Evaluating Urban Tourism', in: Judd, Dennis R./Fainstein, Susan S. (ed.), *The Tourist City*, New Haven/London, Yale University Press, **Featherstone**, Mike (1991), *Consumer Culture and Postmodernism*, London, Sage Publications, **Fiske**, John (1989), *Reading the Popular*, Boston, Unwin Hyman, **Florian**, Bercy (2002), 'The City as a Brand', in: Patteeuw, Veronique (ed.), *City Branding*, Rotterdam, NAi Publishers, **Franck**, Georg (1998), *Ökonomie der Aufmerksamkeit*, Munich/Vienna, Carl Hanser, **Franck**, Georg, (2000), 'Medienästhetik und Unterhaltungsarchitektur', in: *Merkur* 615, Stuttgart, Klett-Cotta, **Franck**, Georg, (2003), 'Mentaler Kapitalismus', in: *Merkur* 645, Stuttgart, Klett-Cotta, **Frank**, Thomas (1998), *The Conquest of Cool*, Chicago, University of Chicago Press, **Gebhardt**, Winfried/Hitzler, Ronald/Pfadenhauer, Michaela (ed.) (2000), *Events*, Opladen, Leske + Budrich, **Giuliani**, Thomas/Kehler, Timm (2002), 'Dynamik ausstrahlen', in: Bauer, Gernot, *Architektur als Markenkommunikation*, Basel/Boston/Berlin, Birkhäuser, **Gladwell**, Malcolm (2000), *The Tipping Point*, Berlin, Berlin Verlag, **Glamour** (2002), 'Erleben Sie das coole Presto-Feeling in Ihrer Stadt', in: http://www.glamour.de/glamour/mode/content/03025/index.php, **Goddar**, Jeannette,

(2000), 'Straßenfußballer', in: *Tagesspiegel* 18.10.2000, Berlin, **Goldman** Robert/Papson, Stephen (1998), *Nike Culture*, London, Sage Publications, **Gunter**, Jukuti T./Inabia, Jeffrey (2001), 'Nikevolution' in: Koolhaas, Rem et. al., *Harvard Design School Guide to Shopping*, Cologne, Taschen, **Häußermann**, Hartmut/Siebel, Walter (1993) 'Die Politik der Festivalisierung', in: Häußermann, Hartmut/Siebel, Walter (ed.), *Festivalisierung der Stadtpolitik*, Opladen, Westdeutscher Verlag, **Hardie**, Adrian (2002), 'presto', in: *Adbuster* No. 44, Nov/Dec 2002, Vancouver, **Hardt**, Michael/Negri, Antonio (2002), *Empire*, Frankfurt a.M./New York, Campus, **Harnisch**, Henning (2000), 'Dribbelorgien im Käfig aus Metall', in: taz 10.07.2000, **Hasse**, Jürgen (1994), *Erlebnisräume – Vom Spaß zur Erfahrung*, Vienna, Passagen Verlag, **Hassenpflug**, Dieter (1998), 'Citytainment', in: *Museumskunde 63*, Deutscher Museumsbund, Berlin, **Haupt**, Florian (2003), 'Bauer auf dem Schachbrett', in: *Die Welt* 12.06.2003, **Hawranek**, Dietmar/Kurbjuweit, Dirk (2001), 'Die Drei Welten AG', in: *Der Spiegel* 9/2001, **Henn**, Gunter (2000), *Corporate Architecture*, Ausstellungskatalog Galerie Aedes, Berlin, **Holert**, Tom/Terkessidis, Mark (ed.) (1996), *Mainstream der Minderheiten – Pop in der Kontrollgesellschaft*, Berlin/Amsterdam, Edition ID-Archiv, **Holert**, Tom (2002) 'Brainware im Strukturwandel', in: Ehmann, Sven/Fischer, Axel/Woznicki, Krystian (ed.), *Sneakers etc*, Eigenverlag/co-op Galerie, Berlin, **Honneth**, Axel (2002), 'Organisierte Selbstverwirklichung', in: Honneth, Axel (ed.), *Befreiung aus der Mündigkeit*, Frankfurt a. M./New York, Campus, **Horkheimer**, Max/Adorno, Theodor W. (1989), *Dialektik der Aufklärung*, Frankfurt a. M., Fischer Wissenschaft, **Huxtable**, Ada Louise (1997), *The Unreal America*, New York, New York University Press, **jargonfile.com**, www.jargon-file.com/jargon/html/entry/hack.html, **Kapferer**, Jean Noël (1994), *Strategic Brand Management*, New York/Toronto, The Free Press, **Katz**, Donald (1994), *Just do it*, New York, Random House, **Kittler**, Friedrich/Kluge, Alexander (2003), 'Das Arsenal der Architektur', in: *Arch+* 164/165, **Klein**, Naomi (2001), *No Logo*, Munich, Riemann, **Klein**, Norman (2001), 'Die imaginierte Stadt', in: Bittner, Regina (ed.), *Die Stadt als Event*, Frankfurt a.M./New York, Campus, **Klingmann**, Anna (1998), 'Architektur als Produkt', in: *Daidalos 69/70*, Berlin, Gordon & Breach, **Klingmann**, Anna (1999), 'adidas-scape', in: *Daidalos 73*, Berlin, Gordon & Breach, **Koolhaas**, Rem (1994), *Delirious New York*, Rotterdam, 010 Publishers, **Koolhaas**, Rem (1997), Generic City, in: Koolhaas, Rem/Mau, Bruce, S,M,L,XL, Cologne, Taschen, **Koolhaas**, Rem (2004), 'Es war ein Verbrechen, den Palast der Republik nicht zu retten', in: *Spiegel Online* 27.04.2004, **Küddelsmann**, Alexa, (2001), *Brand Parks und Corporate Lands als Mittel der Unternehmenskommunikation*, Magisterarbeit, www.diplom.de, **Kupetz**, Andrej (2002), 'Architektur für Marken', in: *Anlage 1/Architektur für Marken*,

Rat für Formgebung, Frankfurt a. M., **Kurbjuweit**, Dirk (2003), 'Weltmacht Nike', in: *Der Spiegel* 27/2003, **La Canna**, Xavier (2001), 'Protesters target Nike ads', auf: www. theage.com.au/frontpage/2001/04/09/FFXUQWU-3BLC.html, **Lasn**, Kalle (2001), 'The Smell of Swoosh - this is not an art project', in: *Adbuster* July/Aug 2001, Vancouver, http://www.adbusters.org/creativeresistance/36/1.html, **Le Corbusier** (1982), *Ausblick auf eine Architektur*, Braunschweig/Wiesbaden, Vieweg/Bauwelt Fundamente, **Leach**, Neil (2000), *Millenium Culture*, London, Ellipsis, **Leach**, Neil (2003), 'Der ästhetische Kokon', unv. Manuskript, **Levin**, Thomas Y. (1998) 'Der Urbanismus der Situationisten', in: *Arch+* 139/140, **Liebl**, Franz (2002), 'The Future of Bricolage', auf: http://notesweb.uni-wh.de/wg/wiwi/wgwiwi.-nsf/name/Future_Bricolage-EN, **Liebl**, Franz / Ullrich, Wolfgang (2002), 'Brand-Hacking', in: *Absatzwirtschaft* 6/2002, Düsseldorf, Verlagsgruppe Handelsblatt, **Lootsma**, Bart (1998) 'Ausblick auf eine reflexive Architektur', in: *Arch+* 143, **Lootsma**, Bart (2001), 'Individualisierung', in: *Arch+* 158, **Lootsma**, Bart (2002), 'Street Soccer oder Mittelfeldstratege', in: *Arch+* 163, **Lunenfeld**, Peter (1998), 'Stim City', auf: www.heise.de/tp/english/inhalt/buch/3169/1.html, **Marconi**, Joe (1993), *Beyond Branding*, Chicago/Cambridge, Probus, **Marcuse**, Herbert (1994), *Der eindimensionale Mensch*, Munich, Deutscher Taschenbuch-Verlag, **Maresch**, Rudolf/ Werber, Nils (2002), 'Permanenz des Raums', in: Maresch, Rudolf/Werber, Nils (ed.): *Raum Wissen Macht*, Frankfurt a. M., Suhrkamp, **Michel**, Kai (2002), 'Raus aus der Tonne, rein in die Fabrik', in: Telepolis, http://www.heise.de/tp/deutsch/inhalt/co/11607/1.html, **Miller**, Daniel (1995), *Acknowledging Consumption*, London, Routledge, **Miller**, Daniel (1998), *A Theory of Shopping*, New York, Cornell University Press, **Mohr**, Rafael (1999), 'Hertha-Ausrüster Nike wirbt mit neuen Methoden um die jungen Fans', in: *Welt am Sonntag* 32/1999, **Mohr**, Reinhard (2002), 'Die Prada-Meinhof-Bande', in: *Der Spiegel* 09/2002, **Montilla**, Armando (2001), 'Identi*-Park', in: Bittner, Regina (ed.), *Die Stadt als Event*, Frankfurt a. M./New York, Campus, **Müller-Schneider**, Thomas (2000), 'Die Erlebnisgesellschaft – der kollektive Weg ins Glück?', in: *Aus Politik und Zeitgeschichte*, B12/2000, **Murphy** Peter/Watson, Sophie, (1997), *Surface City*, Annandale, Pluto Press Australia, **Nikesweatshop** (2001), 'Jamming the Jammers', in: http://www.antimedia.net/nikesweatshop/, **Ohrt**, Roberto (1990), *Phantom Avantgarde*, Hamburg, Lukas und Sterneberg, **Opaschowski**, Horst W. (2000a), 'Jugend im Zeitalter der Eventkultur', in: *Aus Politik und Zeitgeschichte*, B12/2000, **Opaschowski**, Horst W. (2000b), *Kathedralen des 21. Jahrhunderts*, Hamburg, Germa Press, **Packard**, Vance (1961), *The Hidden Persuaders*, Harmondsworth, Penguin Books, **Peretti**, Jonah (2001), 'My Nike Media Adventure', www.thenation.com, **Poganatz**, Hilmar/Schwegmann, Martin

(2002), 'Swoosh in der Volkskammer', in: *Jungle World* 49, Berlin, **Rauterberg**, Hanno (2001), 'Ganz große Fragen am Fließband', in: *Die Zeit* 51/2000, **Rebensdorf**, Alicia (2001a), 'Just Fake It', in: http://www.nowtoronto.com/issues/2001-08-16/news_story2.html, **Rebensdorf**, Alicia (2001b), 'USA: Nike Capitalizes on the Anti-Capitalists', in: http://www.corpwatch.org/news/PND.jsp?articleid=42, **Riewoldt**, Otto (2002), *Brandscaping*, Basel/Boston/Berlin, Birkhäuser, **Ronneberger**, Klaus/Lanz, Stephan/Jahn, Walter (1999), *Die Stadt als Beute*, Bonn, Dietz Taschenbuchverlag, **Roost**, Frank (2000), *Die Disneyfizierung der Städte*, Opladen, Leske + Budrich, **Rousseau**, Naomi (2001), 'A Turkey Votes For Christmas', in: http://www.spacehijackers.co.uk/html/projects/zapa/naomir.html, **Ruby**, Andreas (2000), 'Die Verglasung des Stadtraums', in: Henn, Gunter, *Corporate Architecture*, Ausstellungskatalog Galerie Aedes, Berlin, **Rumack**, Leah (2001), 'Presto, you're cool', in: NOW Magazine 11.07.2001, Toronto, (http://www.nowtoronto.com), **Sadler**, Simon (1998), *The Situationist City*, Cambridge, MA, MIT Press, **Sassen**, Saskia (1991), *The Global City*, Princeton/New Jersey, Princeton University Press, **Sassen**, Saskia/Roost, Frank (1999), 'The City – Strategic Site for the Global Entertainment Industry', in: Judd, Dennis R./Fainstein, Susan S. (ed.), *The Tourist City*, New Haven/London, Yale University Press, **Sassen**, Saskia (2000), 'Hongkong – Shanghai,' in: Vöckler, Kai/Luckow, Dirk (ed.), *Peking Shanghai Shenzhen*, Frankfurt a. M./New York, Campus, **Sattler**, Henrik (2001), *Markenpolitik*, Stuttgart, Kohlhammer, **Schirrmacher**, Joachim (2002), 'Storedesign: Das Leben als Erlebnis', in: *Anlage 1/ Architektur für Marken*, Rat für Formgebung, Frankfurt a. M., **Schröder und Schömbs** (2001), 'Berlin darf gespannt sein', Presseinformation, **Schuchardt**, Read Mercer, (1997), Swooshtika: Icons für Corporate Tribes, in: *re:generation* 3.3., auf: www.regenerator.com/3.3/swoosh.html, **Schulze**, Gerhard (1999), *Kulissen des Glücks*, Frankfurt a. M./New York, Campus, **Schulze**, Gerhard (2000a), *Die Erlebnisgesellschaft*, Frankfurt a. M./New York, Campus Verlag, **Schulze**, Gerhard (2000b), 'Was wird aus der Erlebnisgesellschaft', in: *Aus Politik und Zeitgeschichte*, B12/2000, **Schulze**, Gerhard (2001), 'Inszenierte Individualität. Ein modernes Theater', in: Dülmen, Richard van (ed.), *Der Prozess der Individualisierung*, Vienna, Böhlau-Verlag, **Schmundt**, Hilmar (2000), 'Mörderischer Lauf', in: *Der Spiegel* 49/2000, **Sennett**, Richard (1998), *Der flexible Mensch*, Berlin, Berlin Verlag, **Sellmann**, Matthias/Isenberg, Wolfgang (2000), 'Die Wiederverzauberung der Welten', in: Isenberg, Wolfgang/ Sellmann, Matthias (ed.), *Konsum als Religion*, Mönchengladbach, B. Kühlen, **Snowden**, Paul (2003), 'Representation in the Big City', in: *Shift Magazine*, February 2003, **Sorkin**, Michael (ed.) (1992), *Variations on a Theme Park*, New York, The Noonday-Press, **spacehijackers** (2001), 'Boxfresh Zapatista

Campaign 08/01', in: http://www.spacehijackers.co.uk/html/projects/boxfreshres.html, **Strasser**, J.B./Becklund, Laura (1993), *Swoosh*, New York, Harper Business, **Steinecke**, Albrecht (2000), 'Auf dem Weg zum Hyperkonsumenten', in: Isenberg, Wolfgang/ Sellmann, Matthias (ed.), *Konsum als Religion*, Mönchengladbach, B. Kühlen, **Tilin**, Andrew (2002), 'The Ultimate Running Machine', in: *Wired*, August 2000, **Touristikreport** (2000), 'Opel live', in: www.touristikreport.de/archiv/tba/archiv/freizeitparks/ 650267872777797632.html, **Uhlig**, Günther (2000), 'Die Autostadt in Wolfsburg', in: Henn, Gunter, *Corporate Architecture*, Ausstellungskatalog Galerie Aedes, Berlin, **UPJ-Servicebüro** (2003), Projektbeispiele des UPJ-Servicebüros Berlin, auf: http:// upj-online.de/upj/bdatenb.html#b1, **Weiner**, Clay (2003), 'Wicked trainers', in: *Dazed & Confused*, May 2003, London, **Wenderoth**, Andreas (2002), 'Hauptsache extrem', in: *Geo Spezial*, Berlin/Hamburg, Gruner + Jahr, **Wenz**-Gahler, Ingrid (2002), 'Messestände als Markenräume', in: *Anlage 1/Architektur für Marken*, Rat für Formgebung, Frankfurt a. M., **Wigley**, Mark (1998), *Constant's New Babylon*, Rotterdam, 010 Publishers, **Woznicki**, Krystian (2002), 'Der Turnschuh-Kreislauf', in: Ehmann, Sven/Fischer, Axel/Woznicki, Krystian (ed.), *Sneakers etc*, Eigenverlag/co-op Galerie, Berlin, **Zaero** Polo, Alejandro (1994), 'Order out of Chaos, The Material Organisation of Advanced Capitalism', in: *Design Profil* No. 108, London

# ACKNOWLEDGEMENTS

I want to thank everyone who lent their support during work on this volume, whether through encouragement, critical stimulus, or the possibilities they opened up to me, namely: Hubertus Adam, Regina Bittner, Dorothea von Borries, Matthias Böttger, Francesca Fergusson, Georg Franck, Finn Kappe, Ullrich Kirchhoff, Anne C. Müller, Bernhard Schäfers, Stephan Trüby and Klaus Zillich.

My very special thanks to my doctoral advisor Günther Uhlig, without whose confidence this work would never have been undertaken, and to Bart Lootsma, who strengthened my resolve along the way. Thanks also to episode publishers for their openness and productive collaboration. Thanks finally to Brigitte Speich and Markus Wohlhüter for their marvelous design.

# BIOGRAPHY

Friedrich von Borries, born 1974, studied architecture at the ISA St. Luc in Bruxelles, at the University of the Arts Berlin and at the Technical University Karlsruhe, where he received his PhD in 2004. From 2001 to 2003 he taught urban planning and architectural design at the Technical University Berlin, since 2002 he works as lecturer and researcher at the Bauhaus Dessau Foundation.

He published various articles on architecture and everyday culture in *archplus*, *archithese* and *Bauwelt*. Together with Matthias Böttger he runs spatial tactics – agency for spatial recon and intervention in Berlin.

# , THE LOSE

RS GO OFF."

First Edition 2004
© Friedrich von Borries and episode publishers

episode publishers, Rotterdam
info@episode-publishers.nl
www.episode-publishers.nl

Friedrich von Borries
fb@raumtaktik.de
www.raumtaktik.de

With a preface by Bart Lootsma and an epilogue by Günther Uhlig
Editing: Dorothea von Borries, Gregor Dömling
Translation: Ian Pepper

Images: © 2004 individual copyright owners
Design: substratdesign, Brigitte Speich and Markus Wohlhüter
www.substratdesign.org

Printed by Koninklijke Wöhrmann Zutphen
Printed in The Netherlands

ISBN 9059730143